Copyright © 2014 Jennifer Lee

All rights reserved. No part of the material protected by this copyright notice may be reproduced or utilized in any form, electronic or mechanical including photocopying, recording, or by any information storage and retrieval system, without written permission of the author.

First Printing: 2014
Jennifer Lee
Alberta, Canada

Email: info@thenaturalcarnivore.com
Web: www.thenaturalcarnivore.com

ISBN:

The material in this book is for informational purposes. Should a reader decide to use any such information they do so at their own risk and holds author harmless in any and all legal matters concerning the health of their pets and/or livestock whom they may practice the information upon and with any person(s) who they may share the information with.

The
Inner Carnivore

A guide to species appropriate raw feeding for cats & dogs

Jennifer Lee

**Foreword by
Dr. Patricia Jordan, DVM**

The Inner Carnivore

The Inner Carnivore

Dedicated to all those who have been a part of my learning.

Both two legged and four.

Contents

Foreword by Dr. Patricia Jordan, DVM	**6**
Introduction	**11**
1 Anatomy Dictates Diet	**13**
The point of entry	14
Down the hatch	18
Comparing digestive anatomy	20
Wild brethren	22
2 The Early Days of Feeding Cats and Dogs	**27**
3 Evolution of Pet Food	**30**
Origins of raw feeding	33
Industry organizations	35
4 Processed Pet Foods Impair Health	**38**
Not species appropriate	39
Harmful ingredients	40
Processing	45
Digestibility	48
Recalls	48
Marketing	49
Effects on health	51
5 Sourcing & Storing Raw Foods	**58**
Direct from the farm	61
Road kill	61
Processing a carcass	61
Storing raw food	61
6 What & Where to Feed	**63**
Size of foods	64
Organs	65
Tripe	66
Fat	67
Fish	67
Eggs	68
Raw bones	69
Whole prey	70
Muscle meat	70
Other parts	71
Enhanced meat	71

Freezer burnt meat	71
Expired meat	71
Ground meat	72
Frozen meat	72
Fruit, veggies, grains & dairy	73
Fiber	79
Treats	79
Fresh water	80
Where to feed	80
7 How Much & How Often to Feed	**81**
How much to feed	81
Calculating feeding amounts	82
How often to feed	83
Fasting	84
8 Making the Switch	**86**
Dealing with a refuser	89
Changes to expect	90
Balance over time	91
Detoxification and the healing crisis	91
9 Feeding Puppies and Kittens	**94**
10 Supplements	**96**
11 Knowing the Risks & Dispelling Myth's	**100**
12 Reaping the Benefits of Raw Feeding	**104**
13 F.A.Q.'S	**107**
14 Animal Naturopathy	**113**
15 Veterinarian Visits	**121**
16 Your Path	**123**
References	**126**
About the Author	**138**

The Inner Carnivore

Foreword by Dr. Patricia Jordan, DVM

The Inner Carnivore is a well written book for the public to understand a few concepts about feeding your carnivore companion. The most important concept is that companion carnivores need to be fed a diet that their physiology has thrived on and their anatomy evolved upon for over millions of years.

It is important not to try and reinvent the wheel here but to feed what needs to be fed not just to survive but to thrive in life and vitality. Optimal nutrition is required to be healthy and develop a strong immune system.

Author, Jennifer Lee gets across very well the basic concept that "medical experts" you go to for the truth in health and nutrition advice for the companion carnivores are simply unequipped to deliver this vital information to you. My own experience with having a book handed to me by "ABC Pet Food Company" filled with "their version" of making profitable processed diets for pets under a brilliant marketing scheme is hardly "science". Yet this was the "teaching" I was to receive in veterinary school about small animal nutrition.

The company also sponsored veterinary students for much needed scholarships, gave away pet foods as well as texts and would often spring for pizza or other nutritional foods for listening to their version of how feeding processed foods to pets can be profitable. In the fourth year of veterinary school students begin working in clinics under the supervision of a resident veterinarian. In the clinics all there is to see are the well presented marketing displays of these commercially processed foods. The veterinary student thinks this is the "gold standard" without knowing that profitable marketing enabled these displays to be there by "donation".

Even now, these large corporations whose agenda is to make a profit from selling commercially processed foods are continuing to co opt the medical professionals by "sponsoring" the recommended guidelines for nutrition "with healthy educational grants" for all the leading professional veterinary associations; AAHA, AVMA, WSAVA. These large corporations give money and product to the veterinary schools; they sponsor talks that will even get a licensed veterinarian free CE (continuing education) credits necessary for annual -licensure. It is important that you the consumer know that the seduction of the veterinary medical professionals by big business is just that...business, big business and not science. It starts in veterinary clinics, is embedded in veterinary schools and continues well into the veterinarian's "business" practice when they graduate and even into the yearly guidelines they sponsor and in the availability for continuing education.

The Inner Carnivore provides the very history of how commercially processed foods for companion carnivores came to be and is proof that the "marketing hype" is being disguised as "science". There simply is no scientific foundation, no real science with independent oversight to support the hype behind the bag or the can. Starting with Spratt's Dog Cakes in the latter 1870's and through to the history of how pet food is saving the planet bagging up landfill ingredients the proof is in the pudding so to speak, the pet's pudding of commercially processed foods. The massive recalls on these commercially processed pet foods and treats are not to be overlooked. Safety with commercial pet foods is a delusion. The self regulated industry is bound first to their investment and not to your companion animal.

Just like the important health issue; vaccine recommendations, the pet food nutrition recommendations from your professional health care doctors are very much "marketing disguised as science". Dr. Ron Schultz has said that neither the veterinarian nor the veterinary professors teaching in veterinary school have the education, experience, and training necessary in vaccines, vaccinology or even immunology to even be making vaccine recommendations. I would say the very same situation exists for small animal nutrition. Veterinarians do not learn, they are not educated enough or experienced with vaccines, vaccinology, the immune system, health or even the foundation of health, which is nutrition and should not be making recommendations to the public about these topics. One of my veterinary professionals who does have the right experience is Dr. Richard Pitcairn and he noted over the past 30 some years now that the vaccines and commercial pet food feeding are the largest impediments to health in companion animals.

In veterinary school, you are indoctrinated into the fold and prepped to market things for big corporations, but this does not have anything to do with health. The small animal veterinary doctor becomes very good at profiting along with the drug and commercial pet food companies for advancing their agenda. These practices have a history of precedence and not a foundation of science. It is time that the public understand this and empower themselves to be their own first responder for their family's health care, it must start in the home not in the vet's office amongst the brightly colored attractive displays which are there for one reason, to market products.

The author brings to point that the two factors that decide what you will feed your pet are ultimately determined by the financial resources the customer or client has and the availability of those healthy raw food resources. I would support this statement but interject that unless the pet owner empowers themselves with the truth and learns to recognize the "marketing disguised as science" coming from the commercially processed food corporations advertising and the misguided health care professionals those big corporations have easily co opted then you will miss out on the truth and instead fall victim to the marketing.

It is true that choosing the bag or can for convenience sake is a very easy path to take. However once you have read Inner Carnivore you will learn for yourself why your pet is merely surviving and not thriving. If you take the conventional advice hook, line and sinker, you will have the two largest reasons for ill health in companion animals today, unnecessary vaccinations and the feeding of commercially processed pet foods. This road is the indoctrination into chronic disease not the pathway to health. If you are looking for non-conflicting information, truth based on education, experience and training but not sponsored by any corporation, and then take to heart the information in the Inner Carnivore.

I have been feeding raw foods to my companion animals, advising for my patients, teaching this method in my natural medicine classes for almost 2 decades. My colleagues also have been advising this method of nutrition are very excited to see 80% of all disease issues disappear when feeding carnivore companions appropriately. However, it is very easy to see why the business practices in veterinary medicine would not want healthy pets. Medicine thrives off of indoctrinating your family into the chronic disease cycle and then selling you patent drugs, vaccines, products to keep them in a state of mismanaged chronic disease.

Once you finish the book, you are now empowered, like the rest of us who know the benefits of feeding pets appropriately, you are now the one person that can make a difference and extend that human animal bond for as long as possible. You have the power to make a very healthy companion carnivore all by yourself and not listen to those who discourage you against this goal. I have never met a veterinarian who didn't support appropriate carnivore feeding once performing his or her due diligence into the subjects, actually engaging in feeding their own pets appropriately. We as veterinarians have to do our own due diligence…since our veterinary school training left us flat on content with nutrition other than marketing hype.

About Dr. Patricia Jordan:
A 1986 graduate of NC College of Veterinary Medicine and a 2009 graduate of Kingdom College of Naturopathic Medicine.

Dr. Jordan has been in practice for 26 years and is a practice owner of six different veterinary facilities.

She is the author of *Mark of the Beast Hidden in Plain Sight,* which is full of vaccine induced diseases, deaths and disabilities in people and pets. The book is a landmark text used for naturopathic medicine courses at Kingdom College of Natural Health.

Dr. Jordan is a court certified expert in veterinary medicine and in veterinary vaccine damage. Dr. Jordan is an international speaker on natural health and conventional medicine malfeasance. She teaches a course in Asheville, NC on Natural Medicine for Animals. Currently Dr. Jordan maintains a worldwide consultation practice. Her consultation puts everyone within reach of raising healthy animals without falling victim to the marketing schemes of the medical industry. She is working on a second book titled *Back to the Garden,* a 30 year collection of natural medicines for health and vitality.

Her website at www.dr-jordan.com has a large amount of downloadable information. Dr. Jordan's mission is to restore the principles of Hippocrates, our first Naturopath and empower the client to be the first responder for their family's health and well being. The foundation of health is optimal nutrition and the big secret to reversing disease is to feed the right foods and to avoid patent vaccines and drugs.

Introduction to the Inner Carnivore

When I had my first pets I mistakenly assumed the food I was giving them was healthy. I went to the pet store, purchased the brand of kibble that I thought was most appropriate for my pet and that was it. Does this sound familiar? It never really occurred to me that it was junk food disguised as "perfect pet food".

I became motivated to research pet health when one of my dogs had recurring health challenges that conventional care couldn't get to the bottom of. As a concerned pet owner I took matters into my own hands and began researching to try and find some answers. I thought maybe a higher quality food might help my dog. After diligent study on what the best kibble was (raw feeding was not even on my radar yet) I went and purchased a different bag of food. I did not see any improvements in my dog after changing to this new food. Back to the drawing board I went.

Admittedly, I had heard of raw feeding before, but I didn't understand what it was all about and I didn't personally know anyone who was feeding their pets this way. Ironically, it was while reading a paper authored by a kibble company where I first stumbled across the term "biologically appropriate". For me, that's when the switch clicked. This manufacturer was promoting their grain free food with the idea that a meat based diet is what canine and feline species naturally eat in the wild. But they were selling kibble not the actual raw foods that cats and dogs would truly eat in the wild. If a meat based diet was biologically appropriate why wouldn't I just feed meat then? The more I thought about it, feeding a raw diet made a lot of sense. Why hadn't I realized it sooner? Of course cats and dogs are made to eat raw meat and bones not processed pellets! I was literally like a dog with a bone. I read everything I could find about raw feeding.

As for my dog that was having health issues, once he was changed over to a species appropriate raw diet he blossomed. There was a new energy and vitality about him. Wonderfully, the chronic issues he had been having were eliminated with this change in diet. I do not mean to imply that raw feeding is a "miracle cure" because this is not the case. However, it is the only diet that will promote health by providing all the required nutrients in the appropriate form. What I personally witnessed happen with my dog through this diet change make it very clear to me exactly what the effects of processed diets are having on health. For me, the connection between diet and health had been made.

I woke up to the truth about what cats and dogs should be eating and let me tell you, it does not come from a bag or a can. I left behind most of what I had previously believed to be good and necessary for our pet's health and instead turned towards more natural care. I changed all my dogs and cats onto a raw diet and have never looked back.

Since that time when my eyes were opened I have been on a continuous journey of learning how to promote health and prevent disease in my companion animals. Above all else, our pets do not deserve to be victims of the pet food and pharmaceutical industries. They do deserve the opportunity enjoy a life free of chronic disease.

I hope you find the knowledge and inspiration within these pages to feed your own pets in a way that is in harmony with their species-specific needs.

"Come into the light of things, let nature be your teacher"

~William Wordsworth

1
Anatomy Dictates Diet

In order to understand the nutritional needs of dogs and cats it is helpful to first have an understanding of how their anatomy functions and what this tells us about their natural diet.

Dogs and cats are both classified as belonging to the Order of Carnivora. People like to "label and classify" many things in the world. Animals are no exception. In our process of classifying species as carnivores, herbivores, omnivores, insectivores (and so on) we have perhaps unnecessarily complicated the subject by trying to fit every animal into a pre-defined description. However, each species has its own unique characteristics and needs.

Carnivore feeding habits range from exclusively flesh eating to mainly vegetation. The teeth and jaws of each species show corresponding modifications. Bears for instance are classified as carnivores. Brown, black & grizzly bears have a diet that is 60-70% herbivorous and the dentition of the bear is not surprisingly one of a classic omnivore. [1] They have retained the long canine teeth, peg like incisors and the shearing pre-molars of a carnivore but the molars are squared with round cusps for grinding vegetation. The polar bear however is highly carnivorous. The carnassial teeth are smaller and sharper than those of the brown bear, and the canine teeth are larger and sharper. [2] No matter what we classify an animal species as the individual qualities must be taken into account when determining the optimal diet.

Nature provides all creatures the means to obtain, eat and digest the food that is appropriate to their species. By studying the anatomy of any particular animal we can learn what its natural diet would consist of. Whether that is insects, vegetation, or flesh and whether they need to be able to fly, climb trees, dig in the earth or have excellent vision to obtain their ideal food. Regardless of the label that is affixed to our pets eating habits, their physiology shows us exactly what they should be eating to thrive. Every part of an animal's body works together cooperatively to create the mechanisms needed to obtain nourishment and foster species survival.

The Point of Entry

Carnivores have a wide mouth opening in relation to the size of their head, which affords benefits in the task of seizing and killing prey. Biting force correlates with body size and the average size of the prey compared to the size of the predator. Smaller predatory animals require less bite force as their prey is also smaller. [1]

The shape and qualities of an animal's skull give clues about their habits. Predators (meat-eaters) tend to have forward facing eyes. This feature gives them vision capable of locating and tracking prey along with good depth perception. In contrast, prey species such as deer have larger eyes, which are located on the sides of their heads. Their anatomy is designed to provide good peripheral vision in order to spot approaching predators. [2]

The position of where the jaw muscle attaches onto the skull gives more clues. In carnivores there is a ridge on top of the skull called a sagittal crest. This crest is the attachment site for the powerful muscle that controls the crushing lower jaw. The sagittal crest is quite pronounced in carnivores and less pronounced in omnivores. Herbivores typically have smaller jaw muscles and they lack an obvious crest on their skull. [3]

Teeth are one of the best visual indicators of how and what an animal eats. By examining the dentition you can tell whether the animal is a meat-eater, plant-eater or both. In carnivores the teeth are tall and pointed with sharp crests and cusps for crushing bone and shearing flesh. Cusps are the bony raised points found on the crown of the teeth. In comparison, the teeth of an herbivore are broad, flat and box like to grind up vegetation. Omnivores have a combination of sharp and flat teeth.

Even though a wide variety of animals eat meat on occasion, carnivores are the only mammals that possess specialized carnassial teeth, designed for cutting through meat and bone. [4]

Like other carnivores, the domestic dog and cat have teeth that are shaped specifically to break down meat and bones. Canine and feline teeth are shaped into a point. This allows the animal to seize and dispatch prey, crush bones and rip and tear chunks of flesh. The incisor and canine teeth are used to seize prey, get food into the mouth and to scrape meat off of bone. The premolars and molars prepare food for swallowing by crushing and shearing off chunks. The carnassial teeth (last upper premolar and first lower molar) powerfully meet with a scissor like action to tear and shear meat. [4]

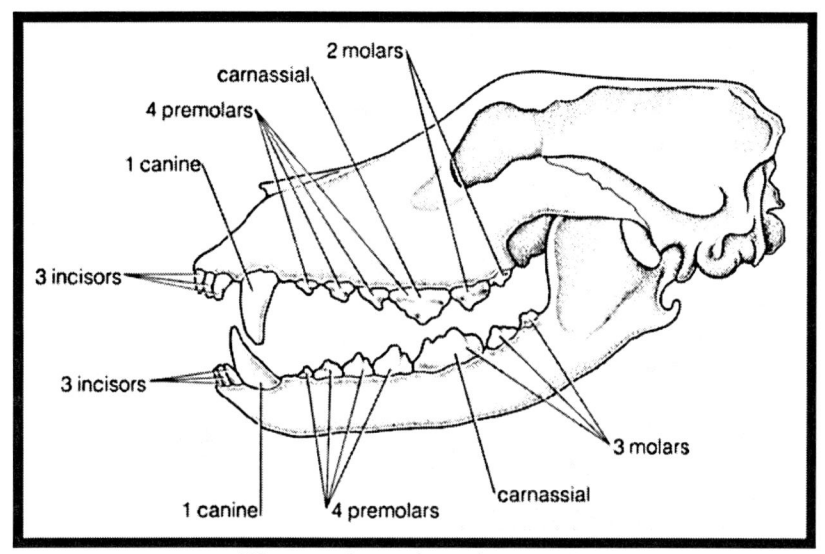

Illustration of canine teeth

Cats and dogs do not possess any completely flat molars and therefore have an almost non-existent ability to grind up and break through the cell walls of any plant matter they could potentially consume. A carnivore's teeth and jaws can be compared to the action of heavy-duty pruning shears, powerful and operating in a single arc of motion. Carnivores do not actually chew their food in the typical sense. They only need to tear off chunks that are small enough to be swallowed. [5] When a dog or cat positions a bone along the side of its jaw to chew it is using its powerful carnassial teeth.

Enamel thickness of the teeth also gives indications of diet. Carnivore tooth enamel is moderately thin and therefore more flexible compared to the tooth enamel of either herbivores or omnivores. Predators are often faced with prey that will violently struggle to free themselves from the jaws of their captor. A more flexible tooth will withstand a greater force upon it before breaking. [6] This is an important feature for a carnivore, as broken teeth would impede continued survival.

The single hinged design of the canine and feline jaw structure limits movement to only an up and down motion. This distinctive motion makes the sharp pyramid shaped teeth work like scissors as the jaw opens and closes. In contrast, the jaws of both herbivores and omnivores are able to move from side to side, and front to back in order to grind up vegetation.

In mammals, the sense of taste helps in the evaluation and consumption of nutrients, and in avoiding toxic substances and indigestible materials. Not all mammals can taste all flavors and the number of taste buds found on the tongue will determine the intensity of the flavor. Dogs are able to taste sweet, salty, bitter and sour flavors. Cats can taste salty, bitter and sour flavors, but are unable to taste sweets. [7] Cats have 470 taste buds [8], dogs 1700 [9], humans 9000 [8], pigs 15,000 and cows 25,000. [10] Cats and dogs seek out foods that contain meat or meat flavors.

The senses of taste and smell help to protect animals from eating substances that will cause them harm. If an animal eats a food that makes them sick it is likely that they will have an aversion to that food in future. It is speculated that both senses also have a role in determining how animals are able to select foods that will meet their nutritional requirements.

The production of salivary enzymes also differs among animals. The enzyme amylase is required to break down plant matter. Herbivores and omnivores both produce this enzyme in their saliva, thus beginning the digestion process in the mouth as they chew. Dogs and cats do not produce amylase in their mouths. They do however produce an enzyme in the mouth called lysozyme that kills bacteria and other harmful pathogens upon contact, a useful trait for a meat eater. [11] Carnivore saliva also functions to lubricate the food being swallowed. If a carnivore secreted enzymes to break down protein and fats in their mouth they would be in danger of breaking down their own body tissues. Instead, their digestion begins in the stomach not the mouth. A mucous lining in the stomach and intestines protects tissues from self-digestion.

The esophagus is the muscular connecting tube between the mouth and the stomach. As food is swallowed it enters the esophagus and travels down through the diaphragm, the muscle that separates the chest from abdominal cavity and is deposited in the stomach. [12]

Down the Hatch

The primary purpose of the digestive system is to break down foods in order to transfer nourishment to the cells. Both cats and dogs have strongly acidic digestive tracts that are short in length and simple in construction. [1] These qualities make for efficient digestion of protein, fat and bone.

Food deposited into the stomach triggers the release of a hormone from the cells in the stomach wall called gastrin. This activates a release of hydrochloric acid, starting the breakdown of food. Contractions of muscular tissues surrounding the stomach mix the food with the gastric juices. [2] The enzymes present in the stomach of carnivores are pepsin (digests protein) and lipase (breaks down fat).

Once the ingested food is mixed with hydrochloric acid in the stomach it becomes semi fluid into a mixture referred to as chyme. The chyme is released gradually from the stomach into the first part of the small intestine, the duodenum. Here, pancreatic enzymes and bile are released. [3] Their function is to break down food particles into their basic components of amino acids, fatty acids and simple sugars.

Carnivores eating a natural diet of animal protein, bones, organs and fats maintain a pH level in the stomach of 1-2. This low pH level is ideal for quickly breaking down protein and neutralizing harmful bacteria. PH is a measure of acidity and alkalinity, rated on a scale of zero to fourteen. Lower numbers reflect an acidic substance (vinegar has a pH of 2), seven is neutral (distilled water) and higher numbers reflect alkaline substances (baking soda has a pH of 9). The type of food eaten affects gastric pH level. [4]

In carnivores, the pancreas is the only source of the enzyme amalyse, which breaks down carbohydrates. In dogs and cats carbohydrates do not undergo any digestion at all until they reach the small intestine where pancreatic amalyse is released and the pH level increases. Canine pancreatic juices also contain antibacterial properties that inactivate pathogens such as escherichia coli, shigella, salmonella & klebsiella. [5]

A normal population of micro flora in the small intestine inhibits colonization by any pathogenic organisms. Beneficial bacteria compete against pathogens for available nutrients, while controlling oxygen concentrations and at the same time producing antibacterial substances. [6]

Nutrients are absorbed in the second and third sections of the small intestine, the jejunum and ileum. Absorption occurs through the intestinal wall and by the hair like projections called villi that line the walls of the intestine. From there the nutrients are transported to the bloodstream to provide nourishment to all the cells of the body. [7] At the end of the small intestine all that remains of the meal is indigestible material, dead cells from intestinal walls, vitamins, minerals and water.

Very little actual digestion occurs in the large intestine in carnivores. The large intestine's main function is the absorption of water and electrolytes. Highly digestible diets had only 1-4%

colonic digestion where starch rich diets (legumes/tapioca) colonic digestibility range from 12 -24%. Bacteria in the colon ferment nutrients, which have thus far escaped digestion and absorption. Total transit time varies dependent on the type of food ingested. [8] The final remains of the ingested food will be passed out of the body in the form of feces.

Microbes in the large intestine (colon) of dogs and cats are able to break down certain types of fiber to varying degrees. This break down is accomplished by bacterial fermentation and produces short chain fatty acids (SCFA). The dog and cat do not derive any significant amount of energy through this process. These short chain fatty acids are however an important energy source for the cells lining the gastrointestinal tract. Research has shown there are benefits to including a source of moderately fermentable fiber in the diets of cats and dogs. The undigested fur, feathers, bone, cartilage, tendon and ligaments of prey form intestinal fiber. [9]

The short, simple and highly acidic intestinal tract of carnivores is not conducive to digestion of carbohydrates or vegetation. If plant matter is eaten most of it will pass through the system with little to no digestion and can even be visually identified in the feces.

Comparing Digestive Anatomy

Unlike carnivores, animals that thrive on a diet of vegetation produce the enzyme amalyse in their saliva and have a much less acidic digestive tract. Also the length of their digestive system is substantially longer and more complex. Vegetation takes quite a bit longer to break down and the digestive tract of herbivores and ruminants therefore needs to be significantly longer. This allows for the cellulose in the plant matter to be fermented and broken down so nutrition can be absorbed. In comparison, mammals subsisting mainly on animal tissue have a simple stomach, colon and small intestine. [1]

- A cats digestive tract is about 4 times the length of their entire body
- Dogs & wolves 5-6 times the length of their body
- Humans 10-12 times the length of their body
- Sheep 27 times the length of their body [2]

Raw meat can be digested and processed in the carnivore's body in as little as 8- 12 hours, whereas plant and vegetable material in an herbivore's gut can take 3-4 days to be processed. [3] The length of the digestive tract compared to body length gives us an idea of how long digestion would take. Vegetation must be fermented in order to break down the cell walls, which takes considerably longer that digesting flesh based food. When eaten by a cat or dog with their short intestinal tract, vegetation simply does not have the chance to be digested. The small intestine of a dog occupies about 20% of the total gastrointestinal area compared to that of about 45% in an omnivore. [4]

Stomach size also differs between carnivores, omnivores and herbivores. The largest stomachs belong to carnivores, comprising about 60-70% of the entire digestive tract. [5] This allows canines to gorge at times when food is plentiful. In the case of wild canines there can be days or even weeks between substantial meals. In comparison, the human stomach, designed for frequent eating, is only about 21-26% of the total digestive tract.

The consumption of meat releases large quantities of uric acid into the system. Uric acid is a toxic substance that is flushed out of the body by the liver. Carnivores produce a special enzyme called uricase, which breaks down uric acid. [6] A carnivore's liver is designed to flush out as much as fifteen times more uric acid than herbivores or omnivores have the ability to, indicating a flesh eating diet. The livers and kidney's of cats and dogs are also proportionately larger in comparison to body size than that of omnivores to accommodate a flesh eating diet. [7]

Canine's and felines have a short, simple and smooth colon and a small caecum. Herbivores possess a large caecum along with a sacculated colon. The caecum is a dead end pouch connected to the colon. Its primary role is cellulose fermentation. It contains a wealth of bacteria to assist in breaking down vegetation. In carnivores the caecum is quite small implying that cellulose break down is not a primary function of a carnivore's digestive system. An herbivores sacculated colon contains sack like pouches, which can accommodate extra volume and prolong the retention of the contents allowing more time for microbial digestion, which is required for plant eaters. [8]

To be healthy, all animals need to eat the foods that are appropriate to their species. Why not feed a horse a rack of ribs? Obviously they are herbivores and meat and bone is not an appropriate food. Yet it has it become commonplace to feed our cats and dogs inappropriately with cooked foods including grains and vegetables. Without human care, our carnivore pets would be seeking out animals to prey on, just like their wolf cousins. Several years ago there was an account of a domestic cattle dog that had become separated from his human family and survived for 4 months on its own by hunting and eating wild goats. [9]

Recognizing that every portion of the anatomy of cats and dogs is geared to a flesh eating diet is the first step to selecting appropriate foods for our companion animals.

Wild Brethren

Before cats and dogs adapted to living with and around humans they relied only upon themselves to find sustenance. For thousands of years Fido and Fluffy hunted and scavenged whatever food they could in order to survive.

Domestic dogs (canis lupus familiaris) are most closely related to the gray wolf (canis lupus). The DNA between the two differs by an exceptionally tiny margin, only 0.02%. [1] This close genetic relationship led the Smithsonian Institute to reclassify the domestic dog from Canis familiaris to Canis lupus familiaris, officially placing the domestic dog under the same family as the gray wolf. There are a variety of subspecies that fall under the Canis lupus classification, mostly different species of wolves and also the dingo.

The gray wolf is the common ancestor of the domestic dog. However, the details of exactly how the domestic dog broke off into a new subspecies are not scientifically clear and a topic of some controversy. Observations about wild wolves provide important information for our domesticated canines.

Professor Wouter Hendriks from the Netherlands believes that feeding behavior in wolves can help to explain a classification of adaptive carnivore for domestic dogs. [2] Like all carnivores, the diet of a wild wolf consists almost entirely of animal protein, fats and bones with their most common prey being deer, moose, caribou, elk, bison, beaver and rabbit. [3] The preferred diet of wolves is typically dominated by whichever large ungulates (moose, elk, and deer) are numerous within their hunting range.

Wolves utilize most parts of an ungulate carcass, which is essential for their nutritional demands. The only portion of the prey that is consistently ignored is the stomach contents. Some berries and grasses are eaten, but are not digested well. All wolves eat grass. Possibly to scour the digestive system and remove worms. [4]

Wolves can maintain themselves on a diet of bones alone for weeks during times without fresh kills. The fatty marrow in fresh bone is a good source of protein and fat. Wild wolves tend to have depleted bone marrow fat levels themselves. This is the last source of stored energy to be used before the animals own muscle tissue is broken down to sustain life. In the absence of food they lose weight daily. However, wolves are adapted to a feast-or-famine diet, and can quickly recover weight lost during long periods of fasting. [5]

Wolf scats collected over 13 years on the Scandinavian Peninsula were analyzed to determine the composition of the diet. The number of scats collected was 2,063. The results of this study found that the primary prey of the wolves was moose, making up 68.9% of the total diet. In total 94.3% of the wolves diet was comprised of prey animals. The remaining 5.7% was made up of insects (0.1%), berries (0.3%), plant material (1.9%), and non-food items (3.4%). [6]

Another 4 year study done on 1,682 gray wolf scats in Arizona and New Mexico had similar results. The average finding over four years determined that 72.8% of the scat was attributed to Elk, 25.6% to other prey species, 0.8% insects and 0.8% vegetation. [7]

A smaller analysis of scat of the Himalayan wolf in Nepal also showed similar results. A total of 91.4% of the diet comprised of prey animals, 4% plant material and 10% unidentified. [8]

If the foods that wild carnivores naturally eat are able to sustain them and support the demands of reproduction in a harsh natural environment surely the same results would be seen in domestic carnivores that are generally protected from the harshness of nature.

Domestic dogs have not evolved to be omnivores. Even though we have changed their outward appearance through selective breeding, their internal workings still function virtually the same as they did thousands of years ago. Remember, the DNA of gray wolves and domestic dogs only differs by 0.02%.

Animals adapt to changes in their environment over thousands of years. A randomly occurring genetic mutation may give an individual animal an advantage over others of its species that will help the animal thrive and reproduce. Natural selection filters out the poorly adapted animals while the ones that possess beneficial adaptations continue to thrive and reproduce. Over a very long period of time a beneficial trait that occurred in one animal can be seen in an entire species, or a new branch of a species emerges. [9]

Dogs will scavenge a variety of food when given the chance. They are opportunistic. This has given rise to the idea that dogs are omnivores. Scavenging foods is a trait that allows them to survive when prey are not available to catch. Scavenging also saves them from exerting vast amounts of energy to hunt and catch prey. In order to increase their chances of survival wild animals must conserve energy whenever possible. Canines do not have quite the extreme carnivore anatomy as cats do. So what does that mean? In times when their preferred food is elusive they are better able to survive from alternate food sources. However, this is not ideal for long-term optimal health.

Ancestors of the domestic cat have been traced back to a wild species, the Middle Eastern wildcat through DNA (Felis silvestris lybica). Wild felines similar in size to domestic cats catch and eat rodents, birds, rabbits, reptiles and insects. [10] Wild cats of similar stature to domestic cats reportedly eat up to 600 grams of food per day. [11]

Wild carnivores hunt, kill and consume nearly the entire carcass of prey animals and our goal with raw feeding is to model that in our pet's diet. Prey animals contain similar ratios of muscle meat to bone to organs. The foundation of the raw diet is based on following the ratio's that are naturally present in the prey of wild carnivores. Based on the body composition of prey animals the whole prey feeding guideline is to provide 10% edible bone, 80% muscle meat and 10% organs.

Wild animals thrive on their natural diets without any assistance from man and have been doing so for millions of years. This is despite the pressures and at times harsh realities of nature. Yet our pets that are exposed to modern processed foods and medicines are experiencing high rates of chronic disease. Surely we can learn something from this comparison.

Assessing the health of animal populations that have been the least influenced by humans and investigating how they maintain their health can provide us many insights. How do wild animals deal with parasites, infections and injuries? Why aren't they regularly succumbing to parasitic overloads or from infectious diseases? How are they out on their own without ever receiving any veterinary treatments?

In wild animal populations it is not unusual to discover that the animals have been exposed to pathogens such as leptospirosis, parainfluenza and brucellosis without developing disease symptoms. To carry the pathogen without developing any symptoms, we can conclude that these animals are in very good health. Wild carnivores do not develop many of the diseases seen in domestic carnivores including dental diseases. [12] When wild animals do get sick the primary reason is due to a strong disruption in their natural environment and or food sources.

Wild animals select foods that provide all their dietary needs despite changing availability and composition of foods. In addition to eating foods that provide a balanced diet, animals also adapt to changing dietary needs. They even change their eating habits in advance of a change of circumstances such as preparing for migration or hibernation. Animals will also seek out specific plants and other substances for their medicinal properties. [13]

"Let food be thy medicine and medicine be thy food"
~Hippocrates

2
The Early Days of Feeding Cats and Dogs

Precisely when and where domestication of the dog occurred is debated and not much is known about the genetic changes that accompanied the transformation of wolves into dogs. Throughout domestication the diet of the dog has largely been dependent on two factors: financial status of its keepers and availability of foodstuffs.

More than 2000 years ago a Roman scholar by the name of Marcus Terentius Varro (116 B.C. – 27 B.C.) wrote the first farming manual: *Rerum Rusticarum Libri Tres (Three Books on Farming)*. Included in this book he advises how to feed dogs being used for herding flocks of sheep. [1]

"The food of dogs is more like that of man than of sheep: they eat scraps of meat and bones, not grass and leaves. Great care must be taken for their supply of food; for hunger will drive them to hunt for food, if it is not provided, and take them away from the flock. They are also fed on bone soup and even broken bones as well; for these make their teeth stronger and their mouths of wider stretch, because their jaws are spread with greater force, and the savour of the marrow makes them more keen."

Gaston III, Comte de Foix (1331-1391) was a great huntsman of his time. He wrote a book about hunting called *Livre de Chasse (Book of the Hunt)*, which included a section on how he took care of the greyhounds he used in the hunt. [2]

"Besides being fed bran bread, the dogs would also get some of the meat from the hunt. If a dog was sick, he would get better food, such as goat's milk, bean broth, chopped meat, or buttered eggs."

This bit of advice implies that milk, broth, meat and eggs were known to be more nourishing to a dog than bran bread was. Further implying that a dog could live off of bran bread with some meat thrown in, but to get over a sickness needed better nutrition consisting of a higher protein intake.

The wealthy have fed their dog's better quality food simply because they had the means to do so. Better foods for both dogs and cats have consisted of flesh based diets. In the 1800's Empress Tzu Hsi of China was said to feed her Pekingese dogs shark fins, quail breasts and antelope milk. European nobility fed their dogs roast duck.

Dogs that were kept by families with limited means were more likely to be fed whatever was leftover from their human caretaker's meals comprised of scraps of bread, vegetables, potatoes, oatmeal, bones and milk. Anything the dog could scavenge or hunt for himself would have supplemented his diet.

An account of feeding sled dogs in 1879 in the Hudson's Bay states that the dogs were fed pemmican, raw white fish, and offal of fish, tallow and caribou. [3] Pemmican is a nutritious raw mixture of fat, meat and berries.

A how-to book from 1900 offered the following advice on feeding dogs:

"Sheep's heads, trotters, and ox noses form a highly nutritious and valuable food, especially for invalid dogs; boiled down they form a glutinous jelly, of which dogs are particularly fond."

"The dog has a natural fondness for bones, independently of which they are of great value to him. One should always be aloud at least once or twice a week."

Sheep's heads and ox noses were commonly fed to dogs in the 1900's. [4]

The diet of domestic cats has a more straightforward history. They were kept primarily for their rodent hunting skills and their diet was comprised mainly of what they could catch. They were efficient at controlling mice which otherwise would consume grains stored by farmers and households.

Cats were revered in ancient Egypt and prized for their ability to control vermin and kill snakes. Italian coins and pottery from 400 B.C. depict cats being fed meat, birds and cakes. Sicilian writings from the first century B.C. describe priests feeding cats meat, Nile fish and wheat flour mixed with wheat kernels soaked in milk. A book on the subject of cat care from the 1900's mentions feeding horseflesh, cod heads, scalded bread and rabbit. [5]

"When morality is up against profit, it is seldom that profit loses"
~Shirley Chisholm

3
Evolution of Pet Food

During the Industrial Revolution of the mid 1800's dog and cat breeding and exhibition shows became a popular leisure hobby of the middle class. Attitudes towards dogs and cats began to change from largely utilitarian to what we now call pets. This change along with the increase in wealth in this time period opened the window for companies to market foods based upon a newly found emotional attachment to animals. The human-animal bond has created a multibillion-dollar industry dedicated to pet foods.

Biscuits, which started out as food for human consumption were advertised to dog owners in England at least as far back as 1792. However, it took a clever man and a patent to make a success from the idea.

In the 1850's a young electrician from Ohio named James Spratt witnessed a ship's crew throwing leftover "ship's biscuits" onto a dock where they were quickly consumed by waiting dogs. This is said to be the inspiration behind the creation of Spratt's Dog Cakes. The biscuits were a mixture of wheat, vegetables, beet root and beef blood. Spratt boldly declared that fresh beef could "over heat the dog's blood" and table scraps could "break down his digestive powers". [1] The biscuits came onto the market in 1860 in England, and then in 1870 Spratt expanded his business into New York. [2]

In 1908 the F.H. Benner Biscuit Company opened. They produced biscuits shaped like bones for dogs. The company was sold to The National Biscuit Company (Nabisco) in 1931 and the biscuit's were renamed to Milkbones. Aiming to get their product into grocery stores they hired 3000 salesmen to promote their product. [3]

Based on advertisements in kennel magazines, Kennel Food Supply Company of Fairfield, Connecticut was the first dog food canner in the United States in 1916. [4]

Ken-L-Ration canned dog food was introduced in the United States in 1922. Horses at this time were plentiful and were being replaced by cars. Due to the abundance, horsemeat was used in canned pet food. After advertising their product on the popular radio show *The Adventures of Rin Tin Tin* the company was breeding and slaughtering 50,000 horses per year to keep up with the demand for their canned pet food. [5]

Hills introduced prescription diets for dogs in 1939. They marketed their so-called therapeutic dog foods through veterinarians. The marketing message conveyed was that feeding pets was complicated and best left to professionals. This is a message that still abounds today. [6]

After seeing what success having dentist endorse their toothpaste the chairman of Colgate-Palmolive used the same strategy for their Science Diet pet food line. Once in practice vets can receive as much as 40% of the profits of pet food sales in their clinic. [7]

During WWII meat and tin were both in short supply. This drove consumers back to dry foods for their dogs. In 1950 Ralston Purina was the first company to use an extruder to make dry dog food. Extrusion was a manufacturing process that Ralston was already using to produce their Chex cereal. The production of enormous bags of dog kibble was in full swing by the late 1950's. Purina's cat chow hit the shelves in 1962. [8]

The Pet Food Institute was founded in 1958 as the national trade association of dog and cat food manufacturer's. In 1964 the PFI launched a campaign to get people to stop feeding their dogs anything except packaged dog food. Their campaign included articles in magazines as well as radio spots about the dangers of table scraps. A culture of dependence was being formed that is still in existence to this day. Companies began labeling their foods as complete, with no additional foods or supplements necessary. Feeding pets "people food" became branded as harmful. At the same time convenience was a big selling point for canned and packaged pet foods.

As more and more processed and packaged foods were being produced for human consumption there were increasing amounts of waste also being produced. Pet foods were a profitable and convenient way to use animal by-products, grain hulls, floor sweepings and egg waste leftover from the human food industry.

Many companies were likely sensing good profits were possible from this emerging market and began adding pet foods to their already existing product lines. By 1975 there was an astounding 1500 different dog foods on the market.

As competition in the pet food market continued to grow we saw foods being labeled as premium, super premium, holistic and natural in order to imply a higher quality product. These words that are used to describe pet foods do imply a certain level of quality to the purchaser but have little actual meaning. Different formulas were developed for young animals, old animals, small breed dogs and large breed dogs. The pet treat market also took off in the 1980's.

The newest option in kibble has been "grain free". This is the industries answer to pet owners questioning the inappropriate use of grains in pet food. Although these foods do not contain grains they do contain carbohydrates from other sources. Grains are carbohydrates, which break down into fiber, starch and sugar. Dogs and cats have no dietary requirement for carbohydrates. Even though these foods may not contain grains the manner in which it is marketed implies it to be free of carbohydrates, which it is certainly not.

In the last decade dehydrated pet foods have become available. This particular method of processing will allow the food to retain slightly more nutrients compared to kibble or canned food. But it is still not an ideal or appropriate food for our carnivore pets.

Origins of Raw Feeding

Although wild cats and dogs have been eating flesh-based diets for millennia, humans chose to veer away from their evolutionary diet for reasons of convenience, availability and due to influences of marketing. However, there have been individuals that have understood the benefits of feeding a natural diet and have done so despite the trends to feed processed foods. Juliette de Bairacli Levy was one of these individuals and is considered a pioneer in the field of natural animal care. She developed a line of herbal products and treated animals with fasting, natural diets and herbs. She published her first book "Complete Herbal Handbook for Farm and Stable" in 1951.

Dr. Pitcairn's "Complete Guide to Natural Health for Dogs and Cats" was first published in 1982 and is now in its third edition. This book covers a wide array of pet health topics and promotes a cooked homemade diet for pets. It includes a list of common health issues along with preventative measures and holistic treatment options.

Ian Billinghurst was one of the first mainstream veterinarians to publish a book that advocated raw feeding. Billinghurst's first book "Give Your Dog a Bone" was published in 1993. His books became quite popular and introduced the idea of raw feeding to a whole new generation of pet owners. His second book "Grow Your Pups with Bones" was published in 1998 and his third book "The BARF Diet" in 2001. Although his books promote the feeding of fruits, vegetables and grains this was certainly a step in the right direction from dry and canned pet food.

Soon there were a few more books being published on the subject of natural pet care and raw feeding. Pat Lazarus wrote: "Keep Your Dog Healthy the Natural Way" and "Keep Your Cat Healthy the Natural Way", both were published in 1999. Martin Goldstein's "The Nature of Animal Healing: The Definitive Holistic Medicine Guide to Caring for Your Dog and Cat" was published in 2000. Also published in 2000 was Martin Zucker's book "Veterinarians Guide to Natural Remedies for Dogs".

Tom Lonsdale's groundbreaking "Raw Meaty Bones" was published in 2001 and "Work Wonders – Feed Your Dog Raw

Meaty Bones" in 2005. Finally a veterinarian is promoting an appropriate diet for our carnivore pets!

We are coming full circle. Hundreds of years ago cats and dogs naturally preyed upon and ate raw unprocessed animals. Then convenient processed foods became available. Homemade cooked diets began to gain popularity, then fresh diets of meat, vegetables and grain. Now the ancestral diet of meat and bones is gaining attention for its appropriateness and health promoting benefits.

Today we have many veterinarians, nutritionists and other professionals that espouse the benefits of raw feeding through a variety of sources. The Internet has allowed for much sharing of information on raw feeding. For the most part this is a good thing. However not everything on the Internet can be relied on for accuracy or completeness.

Industry Organizations

The American Association of Feed Control Officers (AAFCO), the Food & Drug Administration / Center for Veterinary Medicine (FDA/CVM), the United States Department of Agriculture (USDA) and the National Research Council (NRC) all have a part in pet food regulations and standards.

AAFCO formed in 1909 to establish regulations for the animal feed industry, including ingredient definitions, standards for nutritional profiles, and other guidelines. The FDA/CVM approves new ingredients and deals with contamination/recall issues, while the NRC evaluates research and makes nutrient recommendations. The USDA regulates pet food labels and research.

Since the 1940's The National Research Council has conducted research and released reports on the nutrient requirements of cats and dogs. This information is used in part by AAFCO to formulate its minimum nutrient profiles for pet food manufacturers'. The first

AAFCO publication containing feed definitions was a 48-page report sold to feed manufacturers in 1920. AAFCO standards and nutrient profiles are established through collaboration between the NRC and people working within the industry. AAFCO's nutrient profiles are at best an educated guess on the nutritional needs of animals. The intricate chemical composition of whole foods is impossible to fully evaluate using today's analysis methods. Nutritionists are limited by current analytical methods which destroy the natural biochemical's found within whole foods. [1]

In the early 1970's former president Lyndon Johnson asked the NRC to establish minimum nutrient requirements for dogs. This first set of minimum requirements was released in 1974 and was founded upon meat-based ingredients. At this time, the NRC had not included the use of plant based ingredients. In 1985 the first revised guidelines were released. [2]

Laws regarding pet food manufacturing are present, but there is very little enforcement of these regulations. Labeling requirements for pet food are contained in the annually revised *Official Publication* of AAFCO. [3] While AAFCO does not regulate pet food, it does provide regulations and standards for U.S. pet food makers.

For accurate nutrient requirements a large scale and long term study would be needed. Fortunately it has already taken place. In nature wild carnivores have evolved and thrived on a diet of mostly caught and scavenged prey animals. But because this didn't take place in a laboratory we seem to assign little value in this evolutionary experiment.

AAFCO feeding trials test the palatability of food and the appearance of health in the animals eating the foods. An AAFCO feeding trial is 26 weeks in length. There is absolutely no testing, consideration or claims made to the long term effects of foods.

Any nutritional deficiencies or excesses, unless extreme, would infrequently be detectable after a period of 26 weeks. [4]

An animal may lose no more than 15% of its body weight during a six month feeding trial. No mention is made about limits on weight gain even though obese or overweight pets seem to be much more of a problem than underweight pets. The required blood tests at the close of a feeding trial test four values: red blood cells, hemoglobin, packed cell volume and serum albumin. Yet a standard blood test from a veterinarian analyzes more than 25 different blood values. [5] I can't help but wonder why so few blood values are tested.

While feeding trials are sometimes still done today, they are expensive and time-consuming. A standard chemical analysis may also be used to make sure that a food meets the profiles. Chemical analysis, however, does not address the palatability, digestibility, or biological availability of nutrients in pet food.

"Any food that requires enhancing by the use of chemical substances should in no way be considered food"
~John H. Tobe

4
Processed Pet Foods Impair Health

Everything an animal eats affects their health in either a negative or positive way. Kibble and canned food promotes poor health in our pets. [1] Animals need fresh wholesome foods to be healthy, not denatured preserved pellets. The invention of prepared and packaged pet foods, although convenient and advertised as healthy has many negative effects upon physical condition.

As the pet food industry exploded, so have health problems in pets. Ingredients in processed food are not species appropriate and often of very poor quality. The food is loaded with toxins, chemicals, heavy metals and carcinogens and there are deficiencies in nutrients from processing methods and adequate moisture is absent. In essence, processed pet food can be equated to fast food, convenient, but definitely not nutritious.

Not Species Appropriate

Nutrition is the foundation of good health. Our pets need to eat the foods that their species were designed for. This will provide them with all the nutrients to maintain health and vitality. By scientific principles and evolutionary history dogs and cats are carnivores.

Contrary to marketing messages, kibble foods do not help to keep teeth free of plaque. They contribute to gum disease by leaving food remnants on the teeth. Starches abundantly found in processed foods promote bacterial growth in the mouth. Carnivores naturally keep their teeth and mouth healthy by chewing on animal carcasses. This eliminates the need for "dental chew" treats and the brushing of their teeth, neither of which are as effective as chewing on raw meaty bones anyway.

The behavior of your carnivore animal will suffer if not providing them with the opportunity to act out their instinctual gnawing habits. The physical action of chewing and gnawing releases powerful neurotransmitters in the brain providing both physical and behavioral benefits. [1]

All processed foods contain carbohydrates. When dogs and cats eat vegetables and grains as a staple in their diet this inappropriate food stays in their digestive tract longer than species appropriate food would as they struggle to digest it. The pancreas must work overtime to produce abnormally high amounts of enzymes to attempt to digest the plant matter and grains, which ferment in the gut leading to frequent and foul smelling gas.

Because grains are unnatural for carnivores to eat, their immune systems can "attack" this foreign material causing a constant state of inflammation in the digestive tract. Grains metabolize into glucose during digestion. Glucose feeds cancer cells and contributes to obesity and diabetes. Of all these unnatural ingredients our pets are eating, much of it is not digested at all and passes right through their system. This results in large volumes of stinky feces to deal with.

When manufacturing kibble, carbohydrates are needed in order to make all the ingredients stick together in the various pellet shapes. Because of this need, pet food companies decided to market carbohydrates as a nourishing ingredient. The pet food industry spends a lot of money on advertising to make pet owners believe that grains are good for their cats and dogs. Of course grains are conveniently much cheaper for the pet food manufacturers to acquire than meat, which increases their profits.

Many processed foods contain inappropriate amounts of fiber from unnatural plant sources. High fiber plant foods interfere with mineral absorption in carnivores. [2]

When grains and vegetation are eaten this raises the pH level reducing the activity of the digestive enzymes lipase and pepsin. Lipase is the enzyme needed to break down fats and pepsin breaks down protein. Plant proteins found in corn and soybeans do not contain all of the amino acids in the right proportions to meet the dietary requirements of dogs and cats.

When we insist on constantly feeding a cats and dogs grains and plant matter that they were never meant to eat it creates a significant strain on their whole body. There is simply no substitution for proper nutrition. Cats and dogs are designed by Mother Nature to get their nutritional needs met by consuming raw animal based proteins. Without the required nutrients in the appropriate form for the particular species, a state of good health will never be achieved.

Harmful Ingredients

Plump whole chickens, choice cuts of beef, salmon filets, fresh fruits and vegetables and healthy grains. These are the images pet food manufacturers propagate through the media and advertising. This is what the yearly multibillion dollar pet food industry wants consumers to believe they are buying when they purchase their products. However, most processed pet foods are made of poor quality protein, grains and plant matter. Foodstuffs that are labeled unfit for human consumption are used for pet food.

Inside that inconspicuous bag of kibble are the rendered remains of livestock that were not fit for human consumption because they died from unknown causes, were diseased, had cancerous tumors, or were contaminated, rotting or road kill. Hooves, beaks and feathers used in pet food are high in protein but are not easily digested. Commercials show images of fresh wholesome foods going into the kibble yet this is not often the case. Even the foods that start with higher quality ingredients are not much better for our pets due to how they are processed.

Would you knowingly feed your cat or dog other cats and dogs? Yes, that's right, cats and dogs along with zoo animals that have been euthanized are in some brands of kibble. On the label it's identified as "meat and or bone meal", "meat by-products" or "animal digest" or in other words, mystery meat. As per current labeling requirements, the species of animal contained does not have to be disclosed. The drugs used to euthanize those animals are also included and are not broken down through processing. Not to mention Fido's collar, including flea collars and id tags do not get removed before being rendered. [1] In addition to the health concerns this poses, it also brings up ethical questions.

Because of persistent rumors that rendered by-products contain dead dogs and cats; the FDA conducted a study looking for pentobarbital, the most common euthanasia drug, in pet foods. Not surprisingly they found pentobarbital in dry dog food. Ingredients that were most commonly associated with the presence of pentobarbital were meat-and-bone-meal and animal fat. [2]

Nearly all the corn and soy in pet food comes from genetically modified sources. As of 2011 88% of corn and 93% of soy used in pet food in the U.S is genetically modified. There are many reports of livestock deaths after eating GMO crops, in addition to sterility and allergies. One study on rats eating GMO corn showed a wide range of severe health issues and death. The long term health consequences of eating genetically modified foods is not fully understood.

Additives in pet food include emulsifiers to prevent water and fat from separating, antioxidants to prevent fat from turning rancid and artificial colors and flavors to make the product more attractive to consumers and more palatable to their companion animals. Dyes have been known to cause a range of health problems including cancer, hyperactivity and allergies. [3]

In order to halt oxidation and rancidity of fats preservatives such as butylated hydroxyl anisole (BHA) butylated hydroxyl toluene (BHT), propyl gallate, and tocopherol's are used. To prevent mold and bacterial growth, sucrose, propylene glycol, sorbic acid and potassium and calcium sorbates are used. BHA, BHT and propyl gallate are all found to be cancer causing substances.

In order to have a long shelf life, preservatives are used in kibble. There is no such thing as a totally safe preservative. Ethoxyquin is one type of preservative that is currently used in pet foods and it is highly toxic and carcinogenic. Monsanto originally developed ethoxyquin in the 1950's as an anti-degradation agent for rubber. [4]

In studies done on ethoxyquin it was found that dogs were the most susceptible of all species to the negative effects of the drug. Ethoxyquin has been found in the liver and tissues of dogs several months after they had stopped consuming food containing it.

Vitamin E and vitamin C can be used to preserve food, however when exposed to air 99% of the preservative is destabilized unless one of the previously mentioned cancer causing preservatives is also included. [5]

What is really alarming is that if the pet food manufacturer buys ingredients that already include preservatives they are not required to list them on the label. Only if the manufacturer adds the preservatives themselves do they have to include it on the label. Even with diligent research pet owners can't be sure their brand of kibble does not contain these substances.

Kibble or canned food that uses fish and or fish oil is likely to contain high levels of mercury, ethoxyquin and PCB's. Soybeans are commonly found in pet food even though you may not see it listed on the label (it can be listed as "natural flavor"). Soy is a common allergen in humans and probably in our pets as well. Soy also hinders protein digestion and interferes with the ability of red blood cells to intake oxygen. Studies have also implicated soy as a contributor to the occurrence of bloat in dogs. [6]

Processed foods are deeply contaminated with heavy metals. The FDA has tolerance levels for heavy metals in animal feed which is based on the National Research Council's "Mineral Tolerance of Animals". These tolerance levels are significantly higher that what the Environmental Protection Agency deems safe. [7]

Animals that are eating high levels of aluminum, nickel, copper, iron, cadmium, arsenic, mercury, lead and other heavy metals in their food each day will have a serious impact on their health.

Metals prevent the absorption of beneficial minerals by the body, leading to deficiencies. [8]

Every country has different regulations when it comes to food safety and pet food. The origin of the ingredient can affect the quality of the product. Sources (and with it quality) can change on a regular basis.

Since heating destroys many vitamins and minerals, synthetic versions are added back into processed pet food. Yet in their synthetic forms they have reduced digestibility and absorption rates. When a consumer looks at the label they see all the recommended nutrients listed, yet this is no guarantee that the nutrients can be digested and absorbed upon consumption.

A dog's digestive tract is normally very acidic with a pH of 1 to 2. This naturally creates an environment that is inhospitable to most bacteria. Carbohydrates in processed food alter the pH, lowering the acidity level to a more neutral environment (pH 5-6) where bacteria like salmonella and E. coli can grow and flourish. The digestive enzyme that breaks down protein (pepsin) works best at a low pH level and digestion is slowed if the pH level in the stomach is too high. When we feed inappropriate foods we are rendering the animals natural defense mechanisms against bacteria useless and reducing digestion efficiency.

Bacteria and yeast feed on carbohydrates. Potato and tapioca (commonly used in grain free kibble) are high on the glycemic index, meaning they turn to sugar in the body, contributing to obesity and diabetes.

A commonly used variety of the tapioca plant is cassava. Improper preparation of cassava can leave enough residual cyanide to cause acute cyanide intoxication, goiters and cause ataxia, partial paralysis and death. There have been numerous human deaths from eating this plant. The Japanese Ministry of Health now prohibits the use of cassava for human consumption. This sounds like a perfect setting for another huge recall of contaminated kibble making pets ill. [9]

Various kibble products have been recalled due to grain ingredients being contaminated with mycotoxins. Agricultural and storage processes can reduce the risk of mycotoxin contamination but not eliminate it. Ingestion of mycotoxins have been linked to various health conditions in companion animals including liver disease, kidney disease, immune system problems, digestive disorders, cancer and reproductive problems. Acute poisonings can cause sudden death. [10]

Foods in their whole unprocessed forms contain complex mixtures of phytochemicals, vitamins and minerals, which provide a range of synergistic health benefits that are not found in processed foods.

Processing

The ingredients in pet food (livestock, euthanized pets, plus supermarket and restaurant garbage) are sent to rendering plants where they go into a large container and get ground up. Next everything is heated at high temperatures. The heating process completely destroys two of the essential amino acids (tryptophan and lysine) and damages others, changing their composition and rendering them toxic. These specific toxins created from heating protein are often responsible for what's commonly referred to as "allergies" in our pets. [1]

During heating the fat or tallow rises to the top and is used in pet food as "animal fat, chicken fat, etc." Synthetic vitamins, minerals, cereal grains and other ingredients are added into the mix and this ground up stew is pressed through an extruder to remove moisture. At this point there is very little nutritional value left. It's really little more than rendered waste. Then the extruded pellets are heated a second time by baking. Fat must be sprayed onto the finished pellet to make it palatable to our pets.

Canned food uses many of the same low quality ingredients and is also heated at high temperatures using high pressure pasteurization. Wet or canned food begins with ground ingredients mixed with additives. High heat and pressure processing destroys the amino acids methionine and hisidine and well as vitamin B, vitamin C, vitamin A, thiamine, folic acid, niacin and pantothetic acid and damages other nutrients in varying degrees. If chunks are required, a special extruder forms them to look like pieces of meat. The sealed cans are then put into containers resembling pressure cookers and commercial sterilization takes place.

Proteins are vulnerable to heat, and become damaged, or "denatured," when cooked. Damage to protein is progressive with prolonged heating and higher temperatures. [2] Dry food ingredients are cooked twice, first during rendering and again in the extruder. Altered proteins may contribute to food intolerances, food allergies, and inflammatory bowel disease.

Cooking and processing of whole foods also kill enzymes and renders the food devoid of the natural benefits found in raw foods that help with the break down and absorption of nutrients. [3] Every single cell in the body is dependent on enzymes to fulfill the function of unlocking nutrients in foods so that the body can absorb and utilize them. A diet deficient in enzymes affects digestion efficiency. Both the enzymes produced during digestion and those found in raw food serve the same function, digestion. The more our pets are forced to depend only on internally generated digestive enzymes, the more stress that is placed on their systems. When they eat cooked food, which is devoid of enzymes, they can deplete the body's fixed supply, and the enzyme-producing organs will eventually fail. [4]

Cooking alters foodstuffs; cereals and vegetables become easier to digest because the starches in them are partially broken down, but when heated some nutrients are destroyed causing chemical reactions to take place, making them less digestible. [5] Fats when heated can become toxic. [6]

In 1932 Dr. Francis Pottinger began a study on the health effects in cats fed a heat processed diet. Nine hundred cats were studied over the course of 10 years. One group was fed 2/3 raw meat (including organs), 1/3 raw milk and cod liver oil, and another group was fed exactly the same food with the exception that the meat was cooked.

Comparisons between the two groups measured growth, skeletal development, dental health, allergic sensitivity, reproductive efficiency, the level of resistance to infection, and the calcium phosphorus content of their femurs at death.

The group eating raw food showed striking uniformity in their skeletal development, and were resistant to infection, showed no signs of allergies, were friendly and were able to reproduce easily with healthy offspring.

The cats eating the cooked diets commonly displayed deficiency diseases and skeletal changes, heart problems, vision problems, thyroid disease, parasites, infections and arthritis. By the second generation the cats eating the cooked food were unable to produce healthy viable offspring. The third generation kittens were unable to survive past six months of age. The female cats eating cooked meat were much more irritable and sometimes dangerous to handle, while the males were extremely docile and lacked interest in mating.

When the first and second generation cats that had previously been fed cooked food were placed on the raw diet it took four generations to regain a good state of health. Pottinger discovered that once a female cat is subjected to a deficient diet for a period of

12-18 months she will never again give birth to kittens that have completely normal skeletal and dental development. However, if her kittens are then maintained on an optimal diet a gradual reversal and regeneration takes place. [7]

Digestibility

Pet foods claim to include all the required nutrients for our pets. But how much of these artificial nutrients can our pets actual digest and utilize? The manner in which raw ingredients are processed, cooked and stored has an impact on the bioavailability of nutrients.

In an interesting experiment Dr. Meg Smart, DVM at the University of Saskatoon cooked up old leather boots, sawdust and motor oil to find that this concoction "would pass (pet food minimum) standards." [1] But it is obvious that this concoction would not be digestible. Unfortunately for the concerned consumer, information on digestibility is absent from pet food labels.

Biological value can be gauged by the amount of food consumed compared with the amount of waste excreted. Animal proteins are of higher biological value to cats and dogs than plant proteins. Eggs have the highest biological value at 100%, muscle meats 92%, organ meats 90% compared to wheat at 64% digestibility and corn 54%. [2, 3]

Recalls

In 2007 there was a large scale pet food recall. The problem? The food was contaminated with melamine. The U.S. imported 800 tons of contaminated wheat gluten from China, which ended up in over 5300 different pet food products. Melamine is used in the production of plastics, cleaning products and fertilizers and there is no approved use of it in pet foods. Interestingly, when melamine is mixed with wheat gluten it falsely makes it appear as if the wheat has a higher protein level than it actually does. There were over 500 cases of veterinarian reported kidney illness with over 100 deaths associated with this pet food contamination. A self-reporting online database listed the number of deaths at 3600. No matter the actual number, a lot of pets unnecessarily lost their lives because of human greed and negligence. That is completely unethical and downright disgusting. But yet the same problems continue to occur. Toxic foods sit on the shelves even after reports that they are causing sickness and deaths.

July 18, 2012, the Centers for Disease Control and Prevention reported that 49 people had become infected with Salmonella caused from contaminated kibble. [1]

How can we trust the welfare of our pets to an industry with this kind of track record? Pet owners who continue to feed processed foods are playing Russian roulette. When will it be your brand that is named for deaths and illnesses of pets or people?

Marketing

Kibble is sold in veterinarian offices with financial incentives offered to the veterinarians. By selling pre-packaged foods the veterinarians are protected from any possible liability. If clients have problems with the food they go directly to the manufacturer rather than the veterinarian. Besides, most veterinarians have been bamboozled by the pet food industry just the same as pet owners have. Because veterinarians get little to no training on nutrition it is easy for the pet food companies to come in with their biased information and quickly fill that void in their education.

Aspiring veterinarians are given little to no education on evolutionary diets and how the animal's anatomy and physiology relates to their ideal diet. Instead, pet food companies sponsor animal nutrition guidelines, which are provided to veterinary students. As debt loaded students they are informed that selling pet foods is a great way to bring in additional income. So instead of being focused on what will promote the health of their clients they are directed to focus on what will further their financial goals. Pet food company's use and manipulate veterinarian's to be their pawns, to promote their products for them as they have been trained to do.

Veterinary professional organizations from the AVMA, AAHA, and the CVMA allow this practice despite the blatant conflict of interest. In fact these organizations receive monetary sponsorship for their annual conferences, student scholarships, and continuing education requirements.

On average, pet food sales represent approximately 6.3% to 7.1% of total profits in veterinary clinics. The average mark-up on pet foods is 40-45%. To increase sales of therapeutic pet foods one veterinary textbook recommends: *"Make the correct diagnosis and select a food that can be measurably shown to, or perceived to improve the pet's condition or disease management."* [1] I don't know about you but I am not interested in feeding my animals something that is merely perceived to improve upon a health condition!

Commercial pet food is marketed with advertisements directed to pet owners showing a range of healthy and fresh foods, which is first misrepresenting the ingredients and second, visually appealing to the purchaser not the dog or cat. Since it is the owners who are purchasing the food, the advertisements are geared towards them. You never see images of rodents associated with cat food, yet this would be a large component of a cat's healthy natural diet. [2]

Do you feel like you need to be a scientist to understand pet food labels? There are many long and difficult to pronounce ingredients on labels. Trying to actually identify what these ingredients are and if they are safe can be an exhausting process. Plus, the pet food companies are often changing their formulations. Unless you regularly inspect the label you might miss these changes. Because of the regulations on labeling you can guarantee that all the ingredients are not even listed on the package. You may as well not even bother looking at the label. What is the point if it's not a true representation of the ingredients? It's not worth the paper it's printed on.

Pet owners have blindly put an enormous amount of trust into pet food companies. Believing that there are adequate regulations in place to ensure safe ingredients are used, that the food meets the nutritional requirements and is going to maintain the health of our cats and dogs. Wrong! These corporations are taking advantage of the uninformed consumer.

The big pet food manufacturing companies do not have our pet's best interests in mind. It has become pretty obvious that they are much more concerned about the money they are making than the health of pets. Pet owners must understand that the pet food industry is mostly self-regulated. There are very loose labeling requirements giving pet food companies a lot of leeway to be quite vague with the information they include on labels. Companies are not even required to disclose many of the harmful materials present in the food. There are countless deficiencies in the current regulations for manufacturing foods that are even safe for our pets, never mind healthy and nutritious.

Fear is a strong emotion and pet food companies are using it continuously in order to manipulate people to make emotional rather than logical choices. Smart choices are rarely made from a fearful position.

Effects on Health

Every single brand of processed pet food impacts our pet's health negatively. Some brands will carry more risks than others, but the bottom line is that no brand can be considered safe or healthy.

There are a lot of overweight and even obese pets among us these days. They are not receiving adequate nutrition from commercial foods and are overeating to try and obtain the nutrients their bodies are craving. They have dull coats and weepy eyes; poor muscle tone, a bad overall odor and bad breath from tartar build up. They have itchy skin, large soft stinky stools, diarrhea, ear infections, hot spots and they shed excessively. As these animals mature into adulthood problems are often diagnosed in the organs: kidney disease, heart disease, thyroid problems, and liver disease, diabetes, etc. Gone is the sparkle in their eye, then the diseased organ fails or cancer strikes and death looms.

Convenient food in a bag or can is promoted as the best for our pets so it must be true right? Well, no actually the pet food companies have put out such an enormous amount of propaganda to try and make pet owners believe that their foods are the only safe and healthy choices available. They have made themselves out to be the authority on our pet's diet and have been quite successful in deceiving pet owners and veterinarians alike. They have even managed to get into the universities, courting students with financial rewards and teaching their profit driven ideologies, perpetuating the cycle of miss-information.

Could you imagine drinking a protein shake that is labeled as nutritionally complete for every meal, every single day for the rest of your life? How satisfied would you be with this food source? How healthy do you think you would be? And how long do you think you would live? Yet, this thinking is exactly what pet owners have bought into as being wonderful for their pets.

The cycle of disease begins at weaning when the first unnatural foods are introduced. Puppies and kittens weaned onto dry processed food can suffer damage to their immature digestive systems.

The liver produces bile fluid that plays an important role in the digestion of dietary fats. Bile salts are required during digestion to separate fat molecules, exposing more of the surface to digestive enzymes. Bile is not normally excreted from the body, but instead, reabsorbed and recycled by the liver then returned to the gallbladder for future use. When the intestine is scarred and re-absorption is affected the liver must produce additional bile to compensate. [1]

Eating a lifetime diet of processed food (with no naturally occurring enzymes) places a great demand on the pancreas to produce all of the required digestive enzymes, causing the pancreas to become enlarged and inflamed. White blood cells bring additional enzymes to supplement digestion, meanwhile neglecting their primary job to protect the body from invaders. [2] This is but one way that processed foods disrupt the immune system.

A lack of enzymes slows digestion, allowing the harsh chemicals and foreign molecules within processed foods to sit around in the intestinal tract for extended periods of time. This contributes to irritation of the pancreas, liver and intestinal lining, leading to malabsorbtion syndrome and bacterial overgrowth, resulting in dietary deficiencies and diarrhea. [3]

The adrenal glands, exhausted from this sustained effort, may produce cortisol that is biologically inactive. Excessive cortisol production, prescription steroids, intestinal scarring, and the otherwise occupied white blood cells hamper the immune system and allows large protein molecules to pass through the intestinal lining. In response, antibodies are deployed, which memorize the amino acid chains of the large protein molecules, and attempt to destroy them. The antibodies later recognize that same amino acid chain elsewhere in the animals' own body. Unable to distinguish between self and non-self, the antibodies destroy these tissues as well. This process of the animal's antibodies attacking itself due to improper diets is the cause of many auto-immune diseases.

Irritants in processed foods, bacteria overgrowth and medications cause inflammation of the intestinal lining. An inflamed gut is permeable, allowing the passage of partially digested proteins, bacteria and toxins. This can cause allergy like symptoms and lead to inflammation in other parts of the body, skin infections and diarrhea. [4] The particular disorder each animal develops is likely a matter of genetic predisposition. But many of our pets are experiencing the exact same underlying problems. [5]

Many dogs today exhibit some degree of leaky gut syndrome, intestinal bacterial overgrowth and excess cortisol production. They suffer from chronic skin infections, allergies, autoimmune disorders, vomiting, diarrhea, obesity, hypothyroidism and urinary tract infections.

Dogs and cats that are eating diets of high carbohydrate and high plant protein will have a decrease in the acidity level of the stomach. It will progressively become more alkaline to a pH of 4 and above. In this less acidic environment, several key issues arise. The altered pH slows digestion, allows bacteria and pathogens to survive and raw bones are no longer able to be broken down effectively. [6]

Despite the claims by pet food companies, kibble foods do not reduce tartar build up they cause it. This should be blatantly obvious considering that the majority of pets are eating dry food plus "dental chew" treats and are still experiencing dental problems. The sugars (carbohydrates) in pet food feed bacteria in the mouth, which contributes to tartar and calculi, build up. Not to mention bad breath! When periodontal disease arises this not only causes problems in the mouth, but problems with the heart, liver and kidneys as the bacteria from the mouth enters the animal's bloodstream. Many animals affected with periodontal disease will suffer from pain especially when eating. Why spend your money on special chews, toothpastes and dental cleanings when feeding a correct diet of raw meat and bones will give your pet what it needs to have a healthy mouth naturally? [7]

The skulls from captive carnivores fed on soft foods are often highly abnormal. With little work to do, the jaw muscles do not develop to their potential. In these animals the sagittal and occipital crests where the jaw muscles attach to the skull may be lacking. Normal carnivore skulls are heavy with pronounced bony crests to support strong jaw muscle attachments. [8]

It wasn't so long ago that cats were going blind and dying of dilated cardiomyopathy due to a taurine deficiency in their "complete and balanced" cat food. It was only in 1987 that it was discovered that cooked meat was deficient in taurine, while the same raw meat was not deficient. [9] Wouldn't that be a great big clue that cats are meant to eat a raw meat diet rather than cooked? Prior to this discovery the problem was considered idiopathic. I wonder what other health issues that are today considered to be of unknown causes will be attributed to nutritional oversights in the future?

Kibble contains practically no moisture so animals must drink large amounts of water to prevent dehydration. Even minor states of chronic dehydration will promote such problems as bladder and kidney stones, kidney infections, urinary tract infections and high blood pressure. [10] Cats and dogs are designed to eat foods that are high in moisture (flesh) and they often won't drink enough water to compensate for a deficiency. For cats and dogs, lapping water from a bowl is an inadequate method to keep well hydrated. Moisture is our pet's most basic and most necessary requirement as their bodies are made up of over 60% water. When the body does not have the liquids it needs to perform its functions properly it will affect overall health.

In the wild both cats and dogs would get most of their water from their prey. Cats eating dry food do not drink enough water to make up for the lack of moisture in the food because they have a low thirst drive. [11] Dry food contains only 10% moisture compared to around 60 - 70% found in fresh animal prey.

On her website Elizabeth Hodgkins, DVM states the following about diabetes in cats:

"Feline diabetes is not the natural fate of hundreds of thousands of pet cats world-wide. It is, rather, a human-created disease that is reaching epidemic proportions because of the highly artificial foods that we have been feeding our feline companions for the past few decades. Without the constant feeding of highly processed, high carbohydrate dry foods, better suited to cattle than cats, adult-onset feline diabetes would be a rare disease, if it occurred at all." [12]

The stool of kibble fed pets is often fairly soft which contributes to anal gland problems. A firm stool will press against the glands and naturally empty them during bowel movements.

It might appear that your pet is doing fine eating kibble. In very few instances will illness be seen to take hold immediately after eating processed food. Disease is most often brewing in silence long before any outward symptoms appear. The damage is slowly being done by poor living and eating habits, getting worse over time without any visible symptoms until it becomes severe enough that a health issue manifests. Because the effects of diet are not immediately noticeable I believe many pet owners are failing to make the connection, or underestimated the impact diet has on health.

When food is not providing adequate nourishment, it promotes overeating. According to the Association for Pet Obesity

Prevention estimates that over 50% of cats and dogs in the United States are overweight or obese. That translates to 93 million pets. [13] Overweight animals have shorter than expected life spans and increased health risks. [14]

Dogs eating a diet consisting solely of dry dog food have an increased risk to develop a condition known as bloat. Additionally, dry foods preserved with citric acid increase this risk and moistening the food further increases the risk. When treated, bloat is fatal in 30% of cases where the stomach has twisted over itself. [15]

Kibble takes an enormous toll on a pet's body. Since the kidneys and liver constantly filter waste products from the body, they are constantly at work when so many impurities are present.

Wild carnivores do not have the same rates of degenerative and chronic diseases as our companion animals do. The wild carnivore faces dangers from starvation, weather and injury. Yet when we take these wild carnivores and domesticate them they begin to suffer from the same types of disease's as humans. This presents some valuable lessons.

The rates of cancer, allergies, auto-immune disease, liver, kidney and skin problems has skyrocketed in our companion animals. This can directly be attributed primarily to poor diets, vaccinations and a build up of toxins in the body.

Health starts from the inside. Healthy animals resist external pathogens, viruses, bacteria and parasites. The ability to overcome external threats to health should be the norm, but unfortunately the processed diets so many pets eat are making this a rare result. Animals need to be well nourished and free of toxins to flourish.

For better or worse, nutrition is one of the few choices that impact our pets on a daily basis. Make nourishing foods unavailable to any species and they will die, either from direct starvation or from the diseases, germs and viruses that are able to take advantage of the weakened immune system.

"As far as carnivores are concerned, they don't just chase the deer for food, but for food and medicine combined"
~Tom Lonsdale, DVM

5
Sourcing & Storing Raw Foods

Where should you buy health promoting raw meat and bones for your pet? The obvious choices like the grocery store or freezer section of the pet store may not be the best options. Most of the meat sold in grocery stores is not very healthy for our pets or for us. Factory farming and commercial processing makes for unhealthy livestock, which in turn results in unhealthy meat that is depleted of nutrients. Raw pet foods sold in pet stores can likewise not be the best choice either. These foods are typically ground and often have inappropriate fruits, vegetables and sometimes even grains included. Additionally, these types of raw foods can be quite pricey for what you get.

What you want to look for is meat from organic, free range, naturally fed livestock when possible. Higher quality meat can usually be found at butcher shops, directly from farmers and some raw pet food suppliers. Just like our dogs and cats, the living environment and food given to feed animals has a direct effect of their health. If they have exposure to pesticides, pharmaceutical drugs, chemicals or heavy metals these will accumulate in their bones and tissues. When the animals is then processed and fed to carnivore pets (or humans) these same harmful substances will be ingested. Finding quality foods that don't break the bank is achievable.

Searching out other raw feeders in your area and asking where they buy their food from could be your easiest path to sourcing food. Check out the directory of breeders on the Natural Rearing Dog Breeders Association website to find breeders near you. You can also perform a Google search for "natural rearing dog breeders *your city*" or "raw feeding dog breeders *your city*" for example.

Google search is a fantastic tool to find other raw food leads. Try using the following search terms followed by the name of your city or a large city near you:

- Butchers
- Restaurant suppliers
- Meat packers
- Poultry processors
- Abattoirs

Since so many pet owners are realizing the benefits of feeding a natural raw diet, businesses within the meat industry are getting quite used to inquiries for pet food. Some butchers grind up leftover meat and organs for pet food, or they may have whole bones, organs, chicken and turkey backs (a poultry back or frame is the back and rib cage after the breasts have been removed). Occasionally meat that is close to expiration may be available at a substantially reduced price. Custom meat orders that don't get picked up by the customer or errors in meat cutting may also allow for quality meat to be purchased at a reduced price.Try to find meat from naturally grazed animals that are not given hormones or medications. =Younger animals in general will have accumulated fewer toxins to pass on to your dog or cat.

A Google search for *"raw pet food suppliers"* will give you another list of possible sources. Some companies do ship their products. Ethnic markets are a good place to find more unusual products such as chicken feet, tripe, pancreas, spleen, tongue, whole poultry, whole rabbit and cuts of pork, lamb and chevon (goat). If you are located near a large city there is a good chance of finding a raw food co-op.

Do you know anyone who hunts? You can't beat wild venison or other game meats for dogs and cats, that's about as natural as it gets! Ask any hunters you know to save you the parts that they are not using themselves. At the beginning of each new hunting season ask for any of last year's meat that they may be discarding. [1]

Companies that process whole animals have to pay to get the unwanted parts disposed of. These parts will usually consist of meat scraps, bones, fat, and organs, which are all nutritious for carnivore pets. Often you can take these items for free or for a nominal fee. When you go to pick up your haul, be prepared and bring rubber gloves and plastic totes or cardboard boxes and garbage bags. The scraps will probably be stored in barrels or large bins with wheels. You may have to dig around to select the parts that you want or take what has been saved for you and sort through it at home.

It makes sense to develop a working relationship with these companies. Find out how often they would have items available and what days and times would be best for pick-up. Will they separate certain items for you for a small fee? Will they cut up large bones for a fee?

Direct from the farm

If you inquire from farmers, you may find there is availability to get animals directly from them. This might include culled animals, injured animals, or newborns that did not survive. If you do partake in such an activity, be sure to ask if the animal was given any medications recently.

Road Kill

A freshly killed whole deer could feed one dog for quite a while and not cost you a penny. It is an option if you are up for it! First contact the organization in your area that is responsible for clearing away the road kill to let them know you are interested in claiming animals in the future. They will explain the process to you. Always inspect the carcass first. Check for spoilage. Also check for any foreign material from the road or vehicle that may be lodged in the carcass.

Processing a Carcass

The most efficient piece of equipment would be a meat saw. However they are fairly expensive to purchase. A sawzall (reciprocating saw) is a very useful tool to cut up a carcass and purchasing one won't break the bank. That combined with heavy-duty scissors and good sharp knives should get through just about any type of carcass.

Storing Raw Food

A freezer is a must have when feeding raw. Sometimes you will come across an opportunity to purchase a lot of food for very little money. In order to take advantage of these occasions you must have the freezer space available. Having a second freezer that can be plugged in when needed is advantageous. A secondary freezer is also a good back up in case your primary freezer conks out while full of food. [1]

Packaging food into smaller portions before placing in the freezer will allow for faster defrosting. Decide what will be the most convenient way for you to package up food. One bit of advice…labeling the packages is helpful and very much recommended, especially if you use the same freezer for both human and pet food.

Defrosting frozen food to repackage and re-freeze is a safe practice. Bacteria will grow on defrosted meat, but growth will be halted when re-frozen. If you have leftovers from your pet's meal, store in the refrigerator until the next meal time.

Cut meat into portion sizes appropriate for your pets. A digital kitchen scale comes in handy to prep ready meals. Depending on the size of your pet and therefore the size of portions you will be feeding, defrosting time will vary. After some trial and error you will soon discover the usual amount of time it will take for food to defrost. If you have a large lump of food that froze solid you can try dropping it onto a concrete floor. It just might break apart. Otherwise, it will take some time to defrost completely.

For optimal storage keep your freezer at a temperature of -18 degrees Celsius. This temperature will halt activity of micro-organisms in the meat as well as nearly stop potential degradation by the naturally occurring enzymes in whole food. [2]

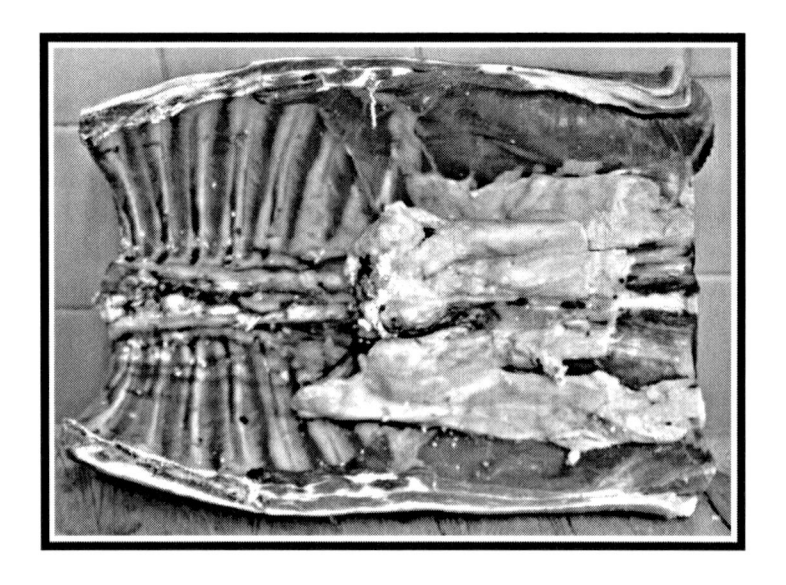

"Food precisely in the form nature gives it to us is always best for the digestion"
~Louis Kuhne

6
What & Where to Feed

Feed a variety of different types of prey animals as they contain different nutrients. A prey animal will be either a herbivore or an omnivore. Here is a list to give you some ideas of different types of meats to feed your cats and dogs:

- Caribou
- Cow
- Deer
- Antelope
- Horse
- Moose
- Sheep
- Pig
- Rabbit

- Kangaroo
- Turkey
- Emu
- Elk
- Ostrich
- Rat
- Duck
- Quail
- Alpaca
- Llama
- Chicken
- Mouse
- Goose
- Pheasant
- Reindeer
- Squirrel
- Goat
- Bison

Size of Foods

The size of your pet will dictate the size of prey or pieces of food they should ideally be given. Whole food that takes work on the animal's part to shear off chunks of meat and crush bones is the most beneficial. The act of working away at a raw meaty bone is great exercise, provides mental stimulation, cleans teeth and starts the digestive juices flowing. A chicken neck would only be appropriate for very small dogs or cats and a chicken quarter or a whole chicken can be fed to larger dogs. The bones of most poultry, rodents, rabbits and fish are completely edible. The neck, rib and tail bones of larger prey animals are generally soft enough for most dogs to consume.

Avoid feeding small pieces of bones. The larger the dog, the larger the meaty bone should be. The dog should not be able to swallow the entire piece whole without doing some work chewing first. This is especially important during the beginning stages of switching a dog over to a raw diet. Dogs especially, that have not had the pleasure of regularly eating this type of food can be very enthusiastic and try to gulp down the food without chewing into pieces first. This can result in choking and regurgitation of food. It will pay off to watch your pet's eating habits in order to gauge if smaller sized items would be safe to feed.

Organs

Organs are very rich in vitamins and minerals and play an important role in the diet. The most common organs fed are liver, kidney, heart, pancreas and lungs. Heart, although an organ is considered muscle meat for the purposes of raw feeding. Raw offal (organ meat such as liver, heart, kidneys, brains, lung, pancreas, spleen) from a variety of meat sources should be fed for one or two meals per week or 10% of the total diet. Pound per pound liver contains more vitamins and minerals than any other part of the animal and should form 5% of the total diet.

Organs in general provide an enzyme-rich mixture of protein, B-complex vitamins, vitamins A and D, vitamin E, some vitamin C, and essential fatty acids EPA, DHA, and ALA, along with minerals such as manganese, selenium, zinc, potassium and copper. Like muscle meat, organs contain a lot of phosphorus and minimal calcium. Although the liver and kidneys are organs that filter toxins and impurities they do not store these substances and are completely safe to feed.

Some dogs do not like the texture of organ meats and lightly searing to change the texture when this food is first introduced will often make it more acceptable to the animal. Other dogs don't tolerate offal in larger quantities well, so it may be best to divide it up and feed a little each day to avoid loose stools.

> **Liver** – source of protein, vitamins A, C, K, B6, B12, biotin, choline, CoQ10, phosphorus, iron, copper, zinc, potassium, folic acid, niacin and trace minerals
> **Kidney** – source of protein, vitamins A, B12, C, D, E and K, iron, zinc, riboflavin, niacin, folic acid, iron, phosphorus and zinc

Heart – source of protein, vitamin A, C, B complex, iron, CoQ10 phosphorus, potassium, essential amino acids including taurine, fatty acids
Lung – source of vitamin, A, C, B complex, phosphorus, potassium, zinc and selenium
Pancreas – source of vitamin B6, B12, C, iron, phosphorus, zinc, selenium and riboflavin
Brain – source of protein, fat, vitamin A, C, choline, phosphorus, magnesium, potassium, sodium, and essential fatty acids

Tripe

Tripe is the four-chambered stomach of a ruminant. If you haven't yet had the pleasure of feeding this food, be warned, it does have a strong odor! Dogs love stinky food and tripe is no exception, it is a favorite food of most dogs. Raw green tripe has long been quoted as being "the finest of natural foods". It should be unprocessed and unbleached, basically straight out the animal. Both wild and domestic carnivores benefit from eating tripe as it contains a very diverse profile of living nutrients including digestive enzymes, omega 3 and 6 fatty acids, vitamin B, probiotics, and phytonutrients.

Raw tripe is considered meat yet has balanced calcium to phosphorus ratio. [1] It is an extremely nutritious and beneficial food if you can get it. Tripe should be sourced from grass-fed animals (not grain fed) to get the maximum nutritional benefit. White tripe found in grocery stores has been bleached and contains little nutrition.

Feeding tripe with its abundance of digestive enzymes and beneficial bacteria works to improve the micro flora in your pet's intestinal tract, which in turn boosts the immune system. The consistency of tripe is fleshy yet tough. Feed in large chunks to promote dental health.

Fat

Fat is an essential dietary requirement of dogs and cats. It provides a natural source of energy and essential fatty acids. Raw fat is a calorie dense food. When switching from a processed diet to a raw diet, build up the fat content in the diet gradually. Too much fat too soon can cause loose stools. We tend to view fat as something that should be eaten minimally. While this may be true for humans, it is a healthy and necessary part of a carnivore's diet.

Dogs eating a high fat diet are better able to burn oxygen and they have more energy. Dogs competing in performance events will have an advantage eating a high fat diet. [1] Hard working sled dogs can burn an astounding 8,000 – 12,000 calories per day. Their diets can contain up to 60% of total calories from fat. In the book *"Ancestral Diets"* the author estimates that wolf diets contained approximately 44% fat. Most domestic dogs are far less active and require less fat in their diet. A range of 10 – 30% depending on the individual dog is typical. [2]

The heart derives 80% of its energy from fats and the brain 70% from fats. Fats are also needed for the absorption of fat soluble vitamins, (A, D & E, K) which are stored in the body. Dogs and cats evolved over millions of years sourcing their energy needs from raw animal fat. It's only in the last 100 years where this has changed to a starch based source. [3]

Fish

Fish can be a great source of omega 3's, which is often a deficient area of the diet. Larger fish generally will accumulate more environmental pollutants. The safest fish with the highest levels of Omega 3's are herring, mackerel, sardines, anchovy, trout, whitefish and wild salmon. Raw fish can be fed for one or two meals per week. You may also opt to feed fish oil such as salmon oil. This supplementation is recommended if the meat you feed is not grass-fed because grain-fed animals lack omega-3 fatty acids. It is preferable to feed smaller whole fish, than portions of a larger fish since the mercury and toxin levels in fish can be a concern.

Salmon poisoning (pacific salmon & other fish from streams in the Pacific Northwest) can be fatal to dogs. Cats are not affected. Deep freezing for 2 weeks or more kills the parasite that is host to the microorganism which causes the poisoning. Avoid feeding farmed fish. The manner in which the fish are raised can be compared to the methods used for commercially raised livestock.

Eggs

In addition to being a great source of protein, eggs also provide many other nutrients. They are a good source of vitamin A & K, riboflavin, folate, vitamin B1, B2, B6, B12, iron, selenium, magnesium, niacin, manganese, zinc, sulpher and fatty acids. The yolk is a source of choline, which is needed for normal brain development and memory. The two carotenoids that give egg yolks their color have been shown to reduce the risks of cataracts and age related macular degeneration. [1] Egg yolks are also one of the few foods that naturally contain vitamin D.

Eggshells provide calcium and can be a useful food for animals that have difficulty eating bones. The shell can be ground up and added to the pet's food. If you are feeding the shell it is best to use organic eggs to avoid any chemicals or wax typically found on commercial eggshells. Pasture raised free range hens produce eggs that contain higher amounts of omega 3 fatty acids.

Inside the shell there are two membranes that surround the egg. These membranes are the richest known source of natural glucosamine, hyaluronic acid, chondroitin sulfate and collagen. These nutrients are needed to build and repair cartilage and connective tissue. If you are not feeding the shell, you can simply scrape out these membranes so your pets can reap the nutritional benefits of consuming them. [2]

Contained within the egg white is a substance called avadin, which is a biotin inhibitor. Biotin is a B vitamin important for cellular growth and for maintenance of healthy skin and coat. The egg yolk however, is rich in biotin. As long as you feed the egg white and yolk together and feed as part of a varied diet there is no risk of your pet developing a deficiency of biotin. [3]

The most advantageous way to feed eggs is raw. Cooking the egg will change the chemical composition and is often a source of allergy symptoms. Eggs are 100% digestible when fed raw. Whole raw eggs with shells have a perfect ratio of phosphorous to calcium.

A study done by the U.S. Department of Agriculture in 2002 indicated that one in every 30,000 commercially produced eggs was contaminated with salmonella. The rate of contamination is very low. In addition to that, our carnivore pets are very well equipped to deal with any such bacteria. Fresh eggs can be stored in the refrigerator for up to 4 weeks. If the eggs smell off when the shell is opened, discard.

Raw bones

Bones are living tissue composed of living cells just like any other part of the body. They are a complex source of biologically balanced minerals, especially calcium, and also copper, iodine, iron, magnesium, zinc, and manganese. The easiest way to provide balanced calcium is by feeding raw meaty bones that have around 10% edible bone.

Common cuts can include chicken backs, wings, necks or whole carcasses, lamb necks, pork necks, turkey necks, pork hocks, pork ribs, ox tails, turkey tails, even sheep or pork heads for the adventurous. If you are feeding meaty parts then you can feed them alone, if your choices are bonier (such as chicken backs, wings or ribs), then you will need to add in additional meat. Basically, you are trying to replicate whole prey, so look at what you're about to feed and visualize the actual bone content. If half or even a third of it would be edible bone, then you know you need to add more meat. Remember you are aiming for 10% bone. The optimum calcium-phosphorus ratio of 1.2 - 1.4 parts calcium to 1 part phosphorus occurs naturally in raw meaty bones. [1, 2]

Bone content in a carcass a will vary considerably depending on the species and breed of animal. The bone content of a goat carcass for example ranges from 12 – 28%. [3] Bone composition of live weight animals: cattle are approximately 10% bone, chicken 22%, pork 9% and turkey 17% bone. [4] The larger animals will contain varying amounts of dense inedible bone.

Whole prey

This refers to the whole unprocessed animal or bird. Depending on the size of the dog or cat, this could be anything from small birds to a large rabbit. Some people feed larger prey and then remove what isn't eaten and store for the following days until the whole prey animal is eaten in entirety.

Muscle meat

Muscle meat is a great source of protein, which contains essential amino acids, the building blocks of your carnivore pet. Muscle meat contains a high amount of phosphorus and minimal amounts of calcium. Free-range grass-fed meat is rich in omega 3 and beta-carotene while intensively farmed grain-fed meat has very little.

Meats are high in phosphorus and bones are high in calcium. When meat is fed with around 10% bone you have the ideal ratios of calcium to phosphorus required by dogs and cats.

Other Parts

Absolutely go ahead and feed the more unusual parts of prey animals such as chicken feet, beef trachea, tails, lung, tongue and brains. The cartilage found in trachea and poultry feet are loaded in natural chondroitin and glucosamine, which help to build healthy joints. Blood contains protein, iron, sodium and moisture.

Enhanced Meat

Enhanced meat has been soaked or injected with a brine solution of water, salt and possible other additives to improve upon flavor and moisture. The product may or may not disclose that it is enhanced on the label. Shoppers can however check the label for sodium content. High sodium would indicate that the meat has been enhanced. Use the USDA National Nutrient Database at the following website: http://ndb.nal.usda.gov/ to check what the normal non-enhanced sodium content for meat is. Feeding enhanced meat is not recommended. It has been reported to cause digestive upset in animals.

Freezer Burnt Meat

Meat that has been in the freezer for some time and is showing signs of freezer burn is sometimes available from friends or family that are cleaning out a freezer. While it is not harmful to feed this to your pet, meat does degrade over time, resulting in a reduction of nutrients. Freezer burn is caused by exposure to moisture and air. So although freezer burnt meat will have reduced nutrition it is not inherently harmful to feed on occasion.

Expired Meat

Both wild and domestic canines will often store meat, digging a hole and burying it for later consumption. This practice does not normally cause them any problems. Healthy dogs should not experience any negative outcomes from eating expired or "off" meat. Cats prefer their meat to be fresh and do not bury food for later consumption. Never feed meat that has mold on it.

Ground Meat

Besides a couple of uncommon medical issues there is no need to grind raw food for our pets. Carnivores are perfectly equipped with their own built in scissors made from their jaws and teeth to break up the food into pieces that can be swallowed. With humans, part of the enjoyment of eating is the textures and shapes of the foods and I'm sure it's similar for our pets. Who would want everything ground up into mush all the time…yuck!

When meat is ground there will be increased oxidation and damage to the nutrients due to a larger surface area exposed to the air and bacteria. This is not to say that one should never feed ground meats. You may have limited options in variety of meaty bones and choose to increase the variety in your pet's diet by adding some ground meats a few days a week. Other times you may come across a great price for a ground product. In some cases a dog with dental problems may not be able or willing to chew through anything but the softest bones.

However, whole raw bones provide many benefits and should be a regular part of a carnivore's diet. The process of eating whole foods is what keeps the teeth free of plaque and the mouth healthy. Save yourself from expensive and unnecessary dental cleanings by feeding whole raw meaty bones regularly.

Frozen Meat

I do not recommend that frozen foods be fed regularly. Most times a wild carnivore eats its food fresh, while it is still warm. A large frozen bone can be a cool treat on a hot day. If your pet does not like a certain type of food you can try feeding it frozen or partially defrosted, as the dog might dislike the texture. Watch that the dog does not get frustrated with the time it takes to work off a piece sized appropriately for swallowing and attempt to swallow it whole. Food eaten frozen can sometimes be rejected by the stomach and regurgitated back up.

Fruits, Veggies, Grains & Dairy

We should be asking ourselves if the dog or cat has the ability to obtain the food on its own accord without the assistance of humans? This will give us a good idea of how appropriate any particular food is. Dogs and cats do not have any desire to graze in grain fields nor have the ability to cook their foods or obtain milk past the juvenile age. If an animal must rely on a human to cook or grind up foods in order for them to get any value from eating it, does it make any sense that they SHOULD be eating it? If they can't obtain it themselves, how appropriate is it?

Some animals, dogs especially seem to enjoy eating raw fruits and vegetables. So why would they eat it if it's not good for them or if they don't need it? Well, people like to eat all kinds of things, many of which are not good for us either, primarily because it tastes good. Dogs do have a more developed sense of taste than cats and many will eat a variety of foods, but this does not mean it's necessarily good for them. Besides, if you were eating the exact same food day in and day out for years on end you would probably eat anything else given the opportunity, just for some variety.

You may have heard the reasoning that wolves eat the stomach contents of their prey (consisting of plant matter) to support the practice of feeding dog's and cat's vegetables and grains. The truth of the matter is that when wolves take down large herbivores they shake out the contents of their prey's stomach before they consume it. Only the stomach contents of small prey eaten whole by wolves are consumed. Wolf expert David Mech states "The vegetation in the intestinal tract is of no interest to the wolves, but the stomach lining and intestinal wall are consumed, and their contents further strewn about the kill site". [1] Unlike omnivores that gain energy from carbohydrates, cats and dogs get their energy from fats. Cats and dogs produce energy most efficiently from fat, and less efficiently from protein or carbohydrate. [2]

Even though some dogs may like to eat vegetables, most of the nutrients are completely unavailable to dogs. Vegetation will pass quickly through a cat or dog without having the needed time for complete digestion and provide little nutrition to the animal.

Humans tend to anthropomorphize their pets, attributing human like qualities and emotions. The same goes for their diet. Fruits and vegetables are very healthy for humans; we require the vitamins and minerals they contain. Carnivore animals do not need fruits and vegetables. They get every single nutrient they need from a diet based on raw animal products. Cats and dogs are even able to produce vitamin C within their bodies, while humans cannot.

Going back to the physiology of dogs and cats, neither has teeth made for grinding plant matter. Their whole physiology is designed for flesh, not plants. Dogs are opportunistic and will eat wide variety of foods if they have access to them. Many species of animals do the same. Deer and elk, which are considered strict herbivores, have been documented eating raw fish, scavenging eggs and nestlings right from bird nests. [3] Eating opportunism is a strategy that allows an animal to survive.

Thankfully there seems to be a general consensus that cats are carnivores. Dogs on the other hand are often referred to as omnivores, especially by pet food companies looking to further their own agendas. Dogs have a marginally longer digestive tract compared to cats, and will scavenge a variety of available foods when unable to catch prey. However, they are certainly not omnivores.

While I don't agree with making fruits and vegetables a regular part of a dogs diet, I understand that sometimes it can take time for the concept of feeding only raw meat and bones to hit home. If you are having a hard time coming to terms with your dog eating only meat and bones and still desire to feed fruits and veggies despite all the evidence, I would advise keeping it to no more than 10% of their total intake. Down the road as your confidence with raw feeding grows you may decide to further reduce or eliminate the fruits and veggies from your pet's diet.

Fruits and veggies should be limited as much as possible to what would be available to them in the wild. Vegetables that resemble green leafy plants that would be available for grazing in a natural environment would be preferred. Green & red leaf lettuce, chicory, escarole, arugula, mustard greens, watercress, dandelion greens and kale to name a few. Stay away from vegetables that are high on the glycemic index such as potato, carrots and corn. Of all fruits, berries are the most appropriate for dogs. Avoid grapes and citrus fruits.

Any vegetables should be lightly cooked or preferably pulped in a food processor for the dog to be able to absorb any nutrients. Vegetables can be mixed in with the meat portion of the food. Fruits however should be fed separately, an hour before or 3 hours after a meal containing protein. When fruit is fed by itself it travels through the system very quickly. If fruit and protein are fed together the fruit can stay in the stomach longer and begin to ferment.

I do not feed any vegetables to my own dogs, but I do occasionally give berries. These would be available for a dog to eat unaided by humans in a wild state. My dogs do browse on grass, preferring the young tender shoots. They also have access to other natural plants including dandelions, which I have yet to witness ever being eaten. They will on occasion eat raspberries right off the bush, but not fallen apples. A domestic dog completely foraging for all its own food may be less choosy on what it consumed in order to simply survive.

AAFCO nutrient profiles as well as veterinary textbooks state that carbohydrates are not essential for dogs and cats, and that no minimum level of carbohydrate is needed in their diets. Dogs and cats are able to synthesize glucose from protein and fat. They will not normally eat carbohydrate besides the small amount that would be in the gut of small prey. However, most commercially prepared pet foods contain substantial amounts of carbohydrate, leading owners to think that this is an acceptable or even required part of the diet.

Dr. David Kronfeld has written, "no carbohydrates need be provided in the diet for pups after weaning or adult dogs, not even for those subjected to hard work. The liver is easily able to synthesize sufficient glucose (from amino acids derived from protein and glycerol derived from fats) for transport in the blood and utilization in other tissues." [4]

A recent study conducted by geneticists from Uppsala University in Sweden was conducted to determine if there were any differences in how wolves and dogs digest starch. The study shows that dogs have more copies of the gene associated with starch digestion than wolves. The dogs (60 from 14 different breeds) had between 4 and 30 copies of this gene compared to wolves, which only had 2 copies. Respected veterinarian Doug Kneuven reviewed the report and spoke to other experts about this study. He came to the conclusion that:

"they do show genetic differences but fail to conclusively prove that these differences mean that dogs "thrive" on a high starch diet".

He goes on to say:

"when it comes to the canine diet, we are witnessing evolution in action. Rare, mutant dogs can somewhat handle the high carb diets we feed them, while the rest of the pets are sickened by them. After analyzing this study, I still think that ancestral diets are best for the majority of dogs." [5]

There are a number of problems that occur when dogs and cats eat grains. Starch rich foods, high on the glycemic scale turn to sugar when consumed. Sugars release insulin, which in turn causes inflammation. Cancers, a leading cause of death in today's pets also feed on sugar. Another issue with sugar is that it removes minerals from the body, leading to kidney damage. [6]

Cats and dogs have had very little evolutionary exposure to high starch foods such as rice, potatoes, peas, wheat and barley. Starch based food produces unnatural swings in blood sugar, taxing the liver as well as both the thyroid and adrenal glands. Unable to deal with the high volume of starch, these organs will show decreased function over time. Veterinarian James Coghlan states that 75% of his patients are suffering from what he calls "carbohydrate disease". [7]

When eaten, grains are mucous forming and provide an ideal environment for parasites to thrive in. Cooked food, especially grain can be interpreted as foreign material in the digestive system. If our pets consume cooked and processed food day after day, protective mucus will form in excess and build up inside the walls of the intestine. [8] Grains also contribute to the formation of dental plaque and tartar on the teeth, as well as bad breath and flatulence.

Dr. Bernard Jensen, in his book "Tissue Cleansing through Bowel Management," writes:

"Mucosal dysfunction occurs when the intestinal mucous lining becomes stagnant and putrefactive. It begins to develop many unfavorable conditions. No longer does it serve the function of facilitating elimination of fecal material. Instead it degenerates in several ways. It can become abscessed, in which case irritations, abrasions, ulcerations and bleeding can occur. Food passage can be very painful. Mucous can dehydrate and accumulate due to increased viscid consistency. This causes layer upon layer to be built up until extreme constipation occurs. This old material becomes a source of infection and toxic absorption, holding many otherwise excreted products. It also greatly inhibits the absorption of nutrients and water, adding to nutritional crisis." [9]

As a result of faulty eating, nature's protective coating, which was designed for occasional use only, inadvertently contributes to ill health. Excess mucus creates a perfect medium for the proliferation of bacteria, viruses, parasites and worms. Autoimmune diseases may develop due to the fact that the immune system has begun to attack the body, instead of harmful microorganisms. Continually eating lifeless, cooked, refined or processed foods devoid of enzymes over stimulates the immune system in a way that compromises its function. [10]

Carnivores derive much less nutrition from plant-based proteins compared to animal based proteins. Animal protein and eggs have a complete amino acid profile, containing all the essential amino acids. Plant proteins do not contain all the essential amino acids required by carnivores. There are 22 amino acids and of these the dog requires 10 different amino acids to be supplied by the diet & cats require 11 from their diet. The liver manufactures the remaining needed amino acids.

Dairy products such as milk, cottage cheese and yogurt are not species appropriate for a carnivore. Besides neonates, this is a food type that is completely unavailable to wild carnivores. Dogs and cats do not digest lactose well and it is a frequent cause of diarrhea.

Dogs and cats do not need to eat fruits and vegetables to get antioxidants, as they are supplied to carnivores through a variety of raw foods. Meat, bones and organs contain vitamins E, A, and C plus minerals associated with antioxidant enzymes.

Fiber

Dietary fiber is a required component of the diet and effects gut health in several ways. It normalizes transit time of food through the gut, alters nutrient absorption and promotes a healthy colon. Excess dietary fiber causes gas and increased fecal output. In processed pet foods fiber is supplied from plant sources, often in the form of cellulose and beet pulp. Fiber can be soluble and dissolve easily in water, insoluble, which does not dissolve or it can be fermentable.

Fiber that moderately ferments in the intestinal tract creates an ideal amount of short chain fatty acids in the colon, which provides fuel to the beneficial bacteria in the gut. A carnivore gets dietary fiber from the prey animals they eat. During the digestion process some contents pass through the intestines partially or wholly undigested such as fur, feathers, collagen, connective tissue, grasses and some bone. Feeding whole prey provides a variety of fiber types in the diet.

One study showed many health benefits including a protective effect on bowel health in captive cheetah's fed a whole prey diet. [1]

Treats

Dehydrated jerky style treats without any chemicals or additives are a great choice for carnivore pets. Look for products that are made by small companies that place a priority on high quality products. Naturally dehydrated bully sticks, cow hooves, trachea, tripe, lung and liver are also good options.

Fresh Water

Water is the single most important nutrient. Animals can survive the loss of nearly all of their body fat and more than half of their total protein, but a loss of only 10% of their total water results in death. [1] About 60 - 70% of the body is water. Pure, fresh water without chlorine or fluoride should be available in a stainless steel bowl or bucket. Water helps to flush out waste products, lubricate the joints and carry nutrients and oxygen to the cells. Water dishes need to be cleaned regularly to prevent the growth of bacteria and algae.

Where to Feed

Feed in quality stainless steel bowls, never plastic. Designate an easy clean up location for your pets to eat. In a crate, on a towel, tile floor or outside are typical choices. Don't be concerned if your pet's food gets dirt on it if feeding outdoors. This is perfectly natural and there are actually beneficial minerals and bacteria in the soil. Use the same handling and cleaning procedures that you would when preparing meat for yourself to avoid any cross contamination.

Be aware that animals being switched to a raw diet can view food items as highly valuable. If you have more than one pet you may want to feed them in separate locations at first to avoid any possible disputes over food. Always keep children away from pets while they are eating.

It is recommended to routinely watch your dogs while they eat, or be in the vicinity. Changing eating habits can be clues that there is a health issue. Make sure one animal is not eating another animal's food if you have more than one pet. Animals can choke and bones can get stuck inside a dog's mouth. Salivating, pawing at the mouth, shaking the head or rubbing the face on objects are signs that a bone has become lodged in the mouth.

"The essence of all disease is the accumulation in the system of waste matter and impurities due to wrong habits of living"
~Joseph A. Boucher

7
How Much & How Often to Feed

How Much to Feed

The total quantity your pet needs to eat will vary with species, breed, activity level and life stage. A good place to start for adult dogs is 2-3% of their body weight fed daily. For example, a 50 lb. dog eating 2.5% of his body in food would eat 1.25 lbs. of food each day. If your dog is overweight, feed less, try 2.0% or 1.5% of their body weight each day. If your dog is in good lean body weight and fairly active, you might start with 3% and see how he/she responds. Very active dogs may need 3.5% to maintain their body weight. Cats and small dogs generally have a faster metabolism and need slightly more food, about 3-4% of their body weight each day. Growing juvenile animals can eat up to 10% of their body weight each day or 2-3% of their expected adult weight. [1]

Calculating feeding amounts:

A 10 pound dog or cat eating 3% of its body weight in food each day would be calculated as follows:

10 x 0.03 = 0.3 of a pound.

For small amounts you can convert pounds to ounces. There are 16 ounces to a pound. (0.3 lbs. x16 ounces = 4.8 ounces)

A 115 pound dog eating 2.25% of its body weight in food each day would be calculated as follows: 115 lbs. x 0.0225 = 2.59 lbs.

Don't get stuck on feeding precise amounts. Checking your animal's body condition regularly is the very best way to determine if their volume of food intake is optimal. Changes in an animal's activity level, age and reproduction capabilities can alter how many calories they need to eat to maintain their weight. You should be able to easily feel your pet's ribs under a thin layer of tissue. Cats and dogs should both have a defined waist. Adjust their portion accordingly or keep it the same if they are just right, it's really that simple!

When putting the diet together you need to consider how much muscle meat, bone and organ your animal needs to be eating. Taking a look at the body composition of prey animals we can discern that they on average are made up of the following: 70-85% muscle meat, connective tissue, cartilage, tendon, skin and fat, 10-15% edible bone, 5% liver and 5% other organs. The larger prey animals are comprised of more inedible bone than smaller prey animals. The long bones in the legs of larger prey (like cows or deer) are very dense as they are made to carry the entire animal's weight. These bones are not edible. Yet a chicken can be consumed in entirety by most dogs. To model a wild canine diet we follow this guideline for our pet's diets.

- 80% muscle meat (includes heart, tripe, connective tissue, cartilage, fat)
- 10% bone (edible bone)
- 5% liver
- 5% other organs (kidney, spleen, pancreas, lung, brain)

How Often to Feed

There is really no hard and fast rule about how often to feed dogs. Wild canines do not have a "feeding schedule", they eat when the opportunity presents. We can vary when we feed dogs and change things up or we can stick to a schedule.

For dog owners, a once per day feeding is common and works well for most people. I do not recommend feeding more than once per day. It benefits the dog to allow the gastro-intestinal tract a rest between meals. It takes energy to digest and if the animal is constantly digesting then its body doesn't have the energy to put towards other tasks, like repairing cells and ridding toxins from its body.

Dogs who are accustomed to being fed on a schedule are talented at telling time. They know when to expect being fed. During this anticipation of food, their digestion systems are already getting prepared. If the food does not appear on schedule dogs can sometimes vomit up a watery yellow-green liquid. This is bile. Bile is released into the first part of the small intestine to help break down ingested fat. But when the anticipated food doesn't arrive, the bile can enter the stomach, causing irritation and vomiting. [1] Dogs that are fed on more random schedules will generally not vomit bile as their digestive system does not automatically gear up at a certain time of day.

You might find it easier to calculate what your dog needs to eat per week. Dogs will eat approximately 21% of their body weight each week (multiply their daily percentage by seven to get a weekly amount). If you are fasting your dog one day per week, then divide the weekly feeding amount by 6 to get a daily amount. [2] Some dog owners prefer to allow their dogs to gorge a couple of times per week and fast for the remainder of the week. In this case the dog might eat up to 10% of its total weekly intake two times per week and fast on the other days.

The frequency that your pet should be fed will depend primarily on their species and their age. Adult dogs can easily go several days between large meals, but a once per day feeding can be easier to manage. Cats can be fed once or twice a day. Younger puppies and kittens need several smaller meals per day.

Fasting

Canine species in the wild fast often. Even when food is readily available wild canines will completely abstain from eating if they are ill. During times of illness they do not need to eat to "keep their strength up", but rather focus all their energy reserves on healing. Digestion requires a lot of energy from the body. When illness or injury strikes, fasting is a way to allow the body to concentrate its energy on the healing process rather than on digestion.

Instinctually, animals can sense when food will not be beneficial to them. This can be seen often among wild animals. When they are hurt or ill they will go off on their own to rest, and abstain from food until they have either recovered or perished. Hunger will dictate when food is again needed. [1]

As caretakers of our companion animals we can use fasting as another tool to promote health. Fasting can be employed to improve health in the following ways:

- Break down and get rid of wastes that have accumulated in the organs, fatty tissues and intestines
- Decreases inflammatory molecules in many different cell types (inflammation underlies many degenerative diseases).
- Clears infections
- Repairs overworked cells, glands and organs

It is perfectly acceptable to feed the dog twice its daily amount one day and then skip the next day's feeding. Or increase the daily ration slightly and fast one day each week. Withholding their food occasionally is not a cruel punishment, but a very health promoting practice. In most cases dogs can safely be fasted one day a week. Be sure to have plenty of fresh clean water available to assist in clearing waste from the body.

Kittens and puppies should not be fasted. If your dog is ill please consult with a professional before fasting them. Cats should never be fasted. They can develop a serious condition called hepatic lipidosis without regular meals.

"We are free to choose our paths, but we can't choose the consequences that come with them"
~Sean Covey

8
Making the Switch

Once you have secured some sources and stocked the freezer it's time to make the switch. Adult dogs can be fasted for 24 hours from their last kibble meal then immediately started on raw food. Most dogs will readily take to the new diet. At first they may be unsure how to actually eat whole pieces of meat and bones. With some time and encouragement most dogs embrace this diet.

With cats it can be more challenging to switch them over as they are generally fussier in their eating habits. It is recommended to take more of a gradual approach when changing a cat's diet. Start with a tiny bit of raw meat mixed in to their usual food and increase over time. You may have to get creative to get them to take to a raw diet at first. Just as we have to learn about the raw diet, so do our pets!

Even though you have read a lot of information about feeding carnivore pets a raw food diet and have thought it sounded very healthy I understand there can still be a particular level of uncertainty about making this change. The reasons behind the raw diet make perfect sense but you may doubt your ability to do it correctly. You may think that you could make your pet ill if you do things wrong. Let me tell you that your pet is more ill RIGHT NOW eating a processed food diet than he or she will ever be eating a raw diet when using a common sense approach. Do not doubt yourself or your ability to provide a raw diet to your pet. [1]

There is absolutely no need to fear feeding a carnivore a raw diet, it is completely natural and is exactly what carnivores have thrived on for millennia. When you begin to understand the agenda of the players in the pet industry you will see that no one but YOU, the owner is going to look out for what is best for your pets. Your pet's life is literally in your hands.

Feeding a raw food diet will take a bit more planning and effort. But once you see the fulfillment your animal receives from eating a natural diet, plus the improvements in their health I'm sure you will conclude that the effort is definitely worthwhile for the rewards that will be achieved.

Keeping a record of food intake and any particular reactions or responses from your animals can be helpful. You may notice a pattern of loose stools right after feeding one type of protein or organ. Or constipation can indicate a meal containing too much bone in the diet.

Pet owners who are new to raw feeding typically have the same questions. All too often, people are not given the information or confidence they need to begin and this is an unfortunate barrier to getting their pet eating a natural raw diet.

Some dogs and cats can handle just about any raw food that is given to them starting from day one, yet others, particularly those that have been on kibble for several years, or who may have an underlying medical condition may need a gentler approach.

Choose a single protein to start off with. This would usually be something that is easy to obtain and an acceptable price, such as chicken. Chicken is generally well tolerated and contains edible bone. Add in other variety as time goes on and the dog is transitioning well. Liver is essential and should be the first type of organ that is fed. A word of wisdom though is to start with very small pieces as it can cause diarrhea in larger quantities.

Start with a section of the chicken breast and cut a piece according to the size of your dog that includes breast meat and ribs. Feed this portion, storing the rest in the fridge for later use. Check your dog's stools. Ideally, you want to see stools that are not too loose and not too firm. If stools are ok with all parts of the chicken fed for several days you can begin feeding a second meat type.

Continue introducing new proteins only after several days of a good stool. Some dogs may object to one type of protein, yet adore another. If you are having difficulty getting your dog to accept chicken for example, try a different meat source and come back to chicken once fully established on raw.

Once your dog is established on raw food you can start to add in a little organ meat. Because liver is an essential part of the diet it is a good organ to start with. Organ meats, particularly liver, can cause loose stools, especially if too much is fed too soon, so depending on how sensitive your dog is, start with a tiny piece and build up slowly to the full 5% of the diet by checking stools at each increase. Repeat the same gradual process for other organ meats.

An animal that has been eating a processed diet is going to have a lowered acidity in its stomach. They will have some difficulty digesting thick bones to begin with, until the acidity of the stomach returns to a normal balance. Fasting for 24 hours prior to the first raw meal will help to begin the process of normalizing the pH. During this adjustment period (usually about one week) it is advisable to feed only small fine bones that will be easier to digest and include a supplement of digestive enzymes.

If you have ever given your kibble fed dog a raw bone only to find that they had trouble digesting it and vomited pieces of bone you are not alone. Unfortunately, when this happens pet owners assume that their pet cannot handle a raw diet. This is not an accurate assessment. Once the pH returns to its naturally acidic state the animal will have no trouble with digesting bones.

Dealing with a Refuser

There are many things we can try for pets that are reluctant to eat the new foods being offered to them. If a dog chooses not to eat the food you have offered, it's okay to pick it up and put it back into the fridge until the next meal. Fasting is perfectly natural and safe for healthy dogs in most cases.

Sometimes breaking up boney foods with a mallet until the animal is more accustomed to the food will help, or running a knife across meaty portions to create grooves and flaps of meat that are easy to grab onto. Most raw foods have less smell that the dry and canned food our pets have been eating. Sometimes lightly searing the food on the outside will be enough to get the animal interested in it.

Cats do need to eat regularly so it can be necessary to mix their old food in with the new food until they adjust to the new fare and gradually reduce the portion of processed food. You can also try warming the food by placing it in a freezer bag and running warm water on it. Remember, processed foods are sprayed with fat to entice the animal to eat. Raw food generally has less smell to attract the animal to eat it. Be patient and give them some time to get used to the new food.

When cats do not eat for a prolonged time their body will tap into stored fat reserves. This puts a strain on their liver starting a disease process called hepatic lipidosis, which causes nausea and vomiting. [1]

Changes to Expect

One of the first things you will notice when changing to a raw diet, is your pets stool. Instead of heaps of very smelly and often poorly formed feces you will now have small, dry stools that hardly smell and will disintegrate into the earth within days. Do not be alarmed if your pet is no longer drinking very much water. Their need for water will be much less due to the high moisture content contained in meat.

You may perceive a new sense of calmness from your pet as they now have physical exercise and mental stimulation as nature intended from the consumption of their food and they are receiving the nutrients that their bodies need to be healthy. As you see more positive changes in your pets your confidence will increase about your choice of diet.

Be aware that your pet may vomit up pieces of bone as they begin this new diet. As long as this is temporary it is not a cause for concern. Your pet must adjust from eating a starch rich diet to meat and bone. This takes different enzymes and can take your pet's body a short time to produce these specific enzymes and for their pH to return to a naturally acidic state. You can add digestive enzymes to your pet's food to make the transition easier.

A raw food diet does not need to be complicated. Keep things as simple as you can, stick to raw animal products and basic supplements when starting out. Gradually as you feel more comfortable and learn more about the natural raw diet you may choose to fine-tune things a little. Before you know it, you will be helping friends and family to get their pets onto a natural diet too!

Balance over time

It is not necessary to meet animal's dietary requirements in one day's food intake. Liver might be fed twice a week, other organs twice a week and bones 5 days a week. You might feed beef 2 days, chicken 3 days, fish one day, lamb 1 day. The next week it could be venison for 5 days and turkey for 2 days. A variety over time is key.

Fat soluble vitamins (A, D, E and K) are stored in body tissues and therefore do not need to be provided in the food daily. Water soluble vitamins (B and C) are not stored in the body. The animal needs a supply each day from the foods it consumes and through internal synthesis.

Cats, and sometimes dogs when fed the same foods for a continued length of time are likely to refuse different foods. They almost become addicted to a particular food after a time, another reason to keep the diet varied.

Balance can occur over time just as we do with our own diet. You don't need to calculate the exact percentages of protein and carbohydrates, or the exact amount of vitamins and minerals in each of your own meals, and you don't have to do it with your pet's meals. If you feed a variety of meats and organs using the 80/10/10 guidelines then it will balance out over time.

Detoxification and the Healing Crisis

You may have heard of dogs and cats "detoxing" when they first start a raw diet. This all depends on the current health levels of the animal, particularly how many toxins it has been exposed to, and especially how many vaccines, heartworm medications, flea preventatives and symptom suppressing drugs they have been given throughout their lifetime.

You may find that the term "healing crisis" conjures up thoughts of a negative state of health, but it actually refers to the process, which leads to an improved state of health. Very simply, a healing crisis can occur when the body is ridding itself of toxins at a faster rate than the body can clear these toxins away.

When the body is unable to clear away waste and toxins at a quick enough rate a sort of toxic traffic jam arises in the body. This can trigger a temporary increase in the severity of already present symptoms in the animal, or bring about the appearance of new symptoms.

The more frequently reported symptoms during a healing crisis are: lethargy, ear and eye discharges, skin irritations, itching, fever and diarrhea. Once the body catches up with eliminating the backlog of toxins and waste, the symptoms exhibited during the healing crisis will subside. The duration and intensity of the healing crisis varies and is dependent on the amount of toxins that the animal has accumulated during its life. [1]

It is essential to understand that the worsening of the animal's symptoms is only temporary and it should be viewed as a very positive sign that purification is happening. It means that the animal is reacting well to the improved diet and its healing mechanisms have been activated. Treating the animal's symptoms during a healing crisis with drugs will only serve to halt the detoxification process that will lead to more serious health issues in the long run.

Being patient and supporting the animal through this process is vital to their future health. If symptoms are severe there are supportive therapies and supplements that can be used to assist the animal through this stage. Consult with an animal naturopath for recommendations on how to best support your animal during this process.

Sitting back and watching your pet experiencing disease symptoms may seem foreign and generate a feeling of guilt for not providing them relief of their symptoms. But being aware that this is the natural manner in which long term healing occurs may relieve some of the owner's uncertainty. Yes, your pet may go through some discomfort, but only if allowed to weather the crisis naturally will a full recovery of health be possible.

"The least I can do is speak out for those that cannot speak for themselves"
~Jane Goodall

9
Feeding Puppies & Kittens

Puppies and kittens have very small stomachs and therefore need more frequent smaller meals than adults. As they grow their stomach capacity increases and frequency of meals can decrease.

During the growth phase the young animal has an increased requirement for protein, energy and calcium than an adult. Therefore, quality, easily digestible food is even more important in young animals. If the food is of poor quality and they are unable to satisfy their nutritional requirements this will lead to poor growth and development as well as reduced immunity. [1]

Puppies should receive about 2-3% of their ideal/expected adult weight split into 3 or more meals per day depending on age. When puppies are four to six months old, they require a great deal of food and a little extra edible bone as they are building their adult teeth and growing rapidly. Do not let puppies get too thin at this important age as their energy demands are tremendous when cutting new teeth. Like puppies, kittens should receive slightly more food for their weight than an adult would eat.

A roly-poly pup or kitten is not healthy, refrain from overfeeding. [1] A study done on 222 German Shepherd dogs noted that 63% of pups that weighed more than the average were dysplastic at one year of age, where only 37% of pups that weighed less than the average were dysplastic. [2] The heaviest pups will have the most stress on the hips while supporting themselves with the hind legs during nursing. In this study it was noted that the heaviest pups were more aggressive and worked the hardest while nursing, and spent the most time feeding. Hip dysplasia is quite prevalent in domesticated dogs, yet it has not been reported in wild carnivorous animals. [3,4]

When teething, young animals will benefit from access to a supply of raw meaty bones. With a means to work their jaws and gums retained deciduous teeth are an unlikely occurrence.

"The food you eat can be either the safest and most powerful form of medicine or the slowest form of poison"
~Ann Wigmore

10
Supplements

If you are able to feed a variety of quality raw foods it will be less likely that any additional supplements will be needed. If the diet is deemed to be inadequate the best solution is to remedy the diet instead of adding supplements to compensate. However, due to intensive farming methods much of our foods have a reduced nutrient content compared to foods that are farmed using more natural methods. Meat products from commercially raised livestock will have fewer nutrients than meat from naturally raised livestock. Soil becomes degraded from intense farming methods, the crops grown in the soil will have decreased nutrients and the livestock raised on those crops will also have decreased nutrients. When supplementing, be aware that many vitamins and minerals work best cooperatively. For instance vitamin D is needed for calcium absorption and zinc is needed to transport vitamin A. Too much copper prevents zinc absorption and too much manganese interferes with iron absorption. [1] Whole foods contain a complex mixture of vitamins, minerals and phytochemicals. It is not so much any single component that provides health benefits but rather the interaction and ratios of these substances as they naturally occur in whole foods. [2]

One supplement that is commonly needed is omega 3's. Commercially raised livestock are deficient in omega 3 fatty acids, compared to their grass fed counterparts. Dogs and cats require long chain omega 3 fatty acids EPA and DHA found in animal sources rather than the short chain ALA found in plant sources. Choose a supplement that uses an animal based source as it will be absorbed more easily and the animal will gain more benefit. Flax oil for instance is high in omega 3's but is poorly utilized by carnivores.

Enzymes are vital in maintaining health and preventing disease. The body's supply of enzymes is not unlimited. Animals subsisting on enzyme deficient foods will eventually deplete their store of enzymes causing disease in the glands and organs. Animals that have previously been eating processed foods and older animals will receive the most benefit from a supplement of digestive enzymes.

Probiotics introduce beneficial bacteria into the gastrointestinal tract and prebiotics encourage the increase of beneficial bacteria. Their use is indicated in a wide range of situations in order to improve the balance of microorganisms and restore or maintain normal gut function. A healthy population of beneficial bacteria in the gut inhibits harmful bacteria, stimulates the immune system, increases the rates of nutrient absorption and can improve the consistency of the stool. [3] Soil-based probiotics are the most species appropriate for cats and dogs.

A common piece of advice dispensed on the Internet is to feed yogurt to pets because of the beneficial probiotics. First off, this is not species appropriate food for carnivore animals and second, it is debatable how many live bacteria strains are actually present. Most commercially purchased yogurt has been pasteurized, which kills off live bacteria. Adding a tablespoon of yogurt to your pet's food is likely not going to provide any benefit to them at all.

One option is to grow your own probiotics using kefir grains. Kefir can be made from both milk and water. The version made from water would be most appropriate for carnivores. You can purchase active kefir grains, which will provide a never-ending supply of kefir probiotic water for your pets.

Due to intensive farming practices many of our foods are deficient in minerals. Zeolites, fulvic acid and bentonite clay are great substances to add minerals back into the body while supporting elimination of harmful toxins.

Kelp is a commonly used supplement that contains beneficial trace elements. According to Kymythy Schultze in her book, "The Ultimate Diet", she states: Kelp contains vitamins A, B1, B3, B5, B6, B9, B12, C and E, plus zinc, biotin, bromine, calcium, choline, copper, inositol, iodine, PABA, potassium, selenium, sodium and sulfur. The iodine content in kelp is very good for glands and organs, especially the thyroid and liver. It can bind with chemical pollutants in the gastrointestinal tract and prevent their absorption by the body. It increases the contractile force of the heart, improves circulation and is often used for hair loss, goiter, ulcers, obesity and mineral deficiency. [4]

With any supplements it is vital to investigate the quality of the product. Many supplements are made from poor sources and contain harmful substances or may be ineffective. Check the ingredient list. Look up in any ingredients you are unsure of. Choose products that have the least amount of non-species appropriate ingredients.

There is a huge array of supplement products available. Consult with an animal naturopath or carnivore nutritionist for species appropriate recommendations tailored to the individual needs of an animal.

"Education is not the learning of facts, but the training of the mind to think"
~Albert Einstein

11
Knowing the Risks & Dispelling Myth's

Pet food companies are involved in a lot of fear mongering about homemade diets. Fear is a very powerful marketing tool. If they can cause people to fear feeding their pets a natural diet the alternative is that they will continue feeding commercial foods. The industry has pet owners feeling like they are backed into a corner with the safest choice being to feed processed foods. Some of the myth's that have been perpetuated about raw diets are: bones are not safe for pets to eat, your dog will get sick from salmonella, your pet will not have balanced nutrition, companion animals who eat raw food are vicious...all these claims are false.

The raw diet is made out to be so very complicated that even pet owners who would like to switch are daunted by all the conflicting information that is available. Understanding the reason behind this big deception will help pet owners to see the truth about what is truly the best diet for our cats and dogs. Nothing in life is without risk. Being aware of possible risks and taking steps to minimize them will be of benefit.

If too much bone is fed in the diet, animals can get constipated. This is easy to avoid by feeding a proper amount of bone.

Prion diseases cover a range of diseases found in different types of prey animals. Forms of the disease such as Chronic Wasting Disease can affect cows, deer, sheep, goats, mink, and other hoofed animals. One of the better-known diseases's being Spongiform Encephalopathy, aka mad cow disease. The brain, eyes and spinal cords of infected animals carry the disease. Freezing does not inactivate prion diseases. The UDSA has prohibited the sale of parts of cattle (over the age of 30 months) that could carry infection (skull, brain, eyes & spine). There is a rare form that can affect cats (Feline Spongiform Encephalopathy). There is no evidence that this family of diseases can affect canines.

You might be told that it is very difficult to ensure the diet is balanced when feeding raw. Although it's not hard to do it is something that raw feeders need to be aware of. A balanced diet is obtained through feeding a variety of protein sources and includes organs, muscle meat, bones, cartilage, fat, connective tissue, skin and following the 80/10/10 guideline.

If you are concerned that your pet is not getting a balanced diet you can get diagnostic testing done to assess the levels of various nutrients present in the blood and the hair. This will give you an indication if something in the diet needs to be changed.

As a culture we need to stop being fearful of bacteria. The process of irradiating meat kills parasites and bacteria as well as killing living cells in the meat, degrading up to 20% of vitamins and minerals at the time and up to 80% degradation during storage. Studies on animals fed irradiated food show increased tumors, reproductive failure and kidney damage. High-pressure pasteurization also inactivates bacteria in food. However, it causes proteins to become denatured and it does not kill bacteria spores. Foods devoid of bacteria are not healthy. Irradiated cat food brought into Australia in 2008 was blamed for the deaths of 30 cats. [1] Cats and dogs are perfectly able to cope with the bacteria naturally found in raw meat.

With any feeding choice there are risks. Animals can choke on bones, but they can also choke on kibble. Depending on your sources of meat it is possible your pet will be exposed to a parasite from eating raw meat, but this is nothing to be concerned about. Since your pet is receiving optimal nutrition is it very unlikely that they will have a worm infestation unless they are otherwise ill. In any case, there are natural worming products available to handle such a situation if it does occur.

Feeding a raw diet will not make your pet vicious or bloodthirsty. Nature designed cats and dogs as predators. If your cat sees a mouse dart by and it chases after and kills it does that make your cat bloodthirsty? No, that is simply a cat's natural instinct and is normal cat behavior. With dogs there are particular breeds that have more of a drive to chase other animals. This is a characteristic that was selectively bred into them enabling them to perform specific hunting tasks. This is commonly referred to as prey drive. With training this characteristic can be encouraged or discouraged. The diet of the dog does not have any bearing of their level of prey drive, as it is a completely independent drive. As strange as it may seem, many dogs peacefully co-habitate with the same species of animals that they regularly eat.

If dogs or cats were not fed by a kindly human then you would expect that they would eventually go and hunt themselves. This could be wild mice, or the neighbor's bunny. Even though we may place value on an animal such as a rabbit because we keep them as pets and we generally oppose "killing". The act of a dog killing a rabbit for sustenance is as natural as a human picking an apple off of a tree to eat. If the fact that your cat or dog is a predator by their very nature bothers you I would perhaps suggest that it is not the right type of pet for you.

"I am drawn to the wild not because it is wild but because it is sensible, logical, ordered, stable, resilient. Wild nature is everything we're trying to regain"
~Carl Safina

12
Reaping the Benefits of Raw Feeding

Appropriate nutrition is nature's ultimate protection against disease. When eating a raw diet, our carnivore pets will have better health, vitality and longevity. They will produce small firm stools with little odor, have a healthy mouth and teeth, a thick soft coat and a strong immune system. The pet owner will have peace of mind knowing there are no hidden poisons in their animal's food. The animal will be more content with the added mental stimulation that comes from eating a whole food diet.

Raw food will be utilized very well by the animal and produce little waste vs processed grain based foods which produce a lot of waste due to poor digestibility and ability of the animal to absorb nutrients from those types of foods. Raw muscle meat has an estimated 92% rate of digestibility, compared to corn at 54%. [1]

Raw foods are therapeutic! Appropriate foods and feeding practices are the only things proven to extend life expectancy in dogs and it can be speculated that the same is true for cats. [2] Puppies and kittens experience initial intestinal scarring and protein infiltration when weaned on to commercial food at an early age. This scarring is the beginning of a downward spiral of poor health as explained in previous chapters. [3]

As you have read, there are only a few guidelines to follow. With time, you will become more comfortable with your pet's new diet and you will start to see the benefits. Feel confident that you will be joining thousands of people who have safely and effectively made the leap to raw and have never looked back.

Natural food promotes natural health and provides the essential foundation of a strong immune system. Around 70% of the immune system cells are found in the digestive tract. [4]

The benefits:

- Animals enjoy their food and look forward to meal times
- Reduced veterinary expenses
- Shiny healthy coats
- No more doggy smell
- Pearly white teeth, healthy gums, no more bad breath
- Dental cleanings & tooth extractions are not needed
- Better concentration with commands
- Less hyperactive with more energy
- Easier to maintain an ideal weight
- Better muscle tone

- Smaller stools
- Creates a stronger, healthier immune system
- More mental stimulation, helps to ease boredom & destructive behavior
- Parasites are prevented by a healthy system
- It's cheaper in the long run if you find good sources and buy wisely
- Life expectancy of your pet increases
- Peace of mind knowing there are no harmful substances in the food
- Quality of life increases with less chances of chronic disease developing
- Superior brain development, increased intelligence and mental focus
- Provides health benefits to nursing offspring
- Reduced cancer risk
- More enjoyment of your pet, less stress with fewer if any health issues to deal with

"Facts do not cease to exist because they are ignored"
~Aldous Huxley

13
F.A.Q.'s

Aren't bones a hazard to my pet?

Cats and dogs can choke on bones. But they can also choke on kibble. Introduce larger raw meaty bones that must be chewed to be swallowed. Be sure to monitor your pet at meal times. Never feed cooked or smoked bones of any type. When bones are cooked they become hard and brittle and are dangerous for the dog as they can splinter and pierce the stomach or intestines. Raw bones are soft enough to bend and digest easily. Dogs and cats are carnivores and are designed to digest raw meat and bones.

Barring a few medical conditions, dogs should be fed whole meaty bones/carcasses. This gives the most benefit to keep teeth clean, works the neck and jaw muscles and provides mental stimulation. Feed a nice meaty bone a couple of times per week, daily if possible. Witnessing how much enjoyment and satisfaction your pet receives from chewing a raw meaty bone you will begin to understand how it is a very important part of the diet. Not to mention it just might save your possessions from being chewed.

My pet is having less frequent bowel movements and they turn white. Is this normal?

Yes, this is completely normal for a raw fed pet. Your animal is able to more readily digest and now utilize the contents of the food, thus, less waste. The bone content accounts for the stool turning white. If you notice your pet straining while eliminating, you can reduce the amount of bone you are feeding. However, a small amount of straining can help express the anal glands, which would otherwise be a service you would pay your vet or groomer for.

Can bacteria on raw meat make my dog or family sick?

When it comes to handling raw chicken, or any other raw meat, common sense is in order. Just like when you prepare meat for your family, proper sanitation techniques should be followed. Keep food bowls clean by regular washing or by feeding the dog outside on the ground. A little dirt on your dog's food is not a problem.

The acidity level in the canine stomach is very high, creating a very inhospitable environment for bacteria. Because ingested food travels through the entire system so fast, any bacteria still remaining will not get the chance to become established and cause illness. Feeding a raw food diet will actually protect your dog or cat from bacterial contamination. Dogs that eat processed foods are even more likely to shed salmonella bacteria in their feces than are dogs that eat raw food.

Even without apparent symptoms of illness 36% of healthy dogs and 18% of cats carry salmonella in their digestive tract and may shed the bacterium. [1, 2, 3]

Work done at the Ohio State University with 71 dogs showed that 18% of the dogs tested for salmonella were positive. [4] Further studies were conducted in an attempt to infect several of the dogs with Salmonella Typhimurium and Salmonella Enteritidis. The dogs were intentionally dosed with Salmonella either through their food or via a stomach tube and monitored for signs of infection. Organisms were recovered in all of the dog's feces but tested negative three to eight days later. None of the animals showed a clinical state of infection or any evidence of ill effect. [4] In order for salmonella to cause a systemic infection fed via the oral route the bacterium must adapt to the acidic environment it encounters in the stomach and then resist being killed by the white blood cells of the immune system. [3]

Can I feed table scraps?

Considering that most if not all table scraps will consist of inappropriate foods for dogs and cats it's definitely not the best thing to be feeding them. When we change our mindset and look at table scraps as unnecessary and unhealthy for carnivore pets we see that we are not doing them any favors by sharing our food with them. However, a bite off of our plate once in a while will have a minimal impact on their overall health.

Can feeding a raw diet reduce the risk of bloat in my dog?

The chances of bloat are much less to occur in a raw fed dog compared to one eating kibble. It is quite rare for a dog to bloat when they are eating a raw diet. Firstly, raw food doesn't swell in the stomach like kibble, which can cause problems. The second thing is that most dogs eat more slowly when they are eating raw food compared to the "inhale" style eating that dogs use when they are eating kibble. Because they aren't inhaling their food, less air is sucked into the stomach. Another reason is that chewing allows the dog's body to prepare for digestion. The necessary juices and acids are released slightly prior to the "deposit" of food into the stomach. This condition is rare in nature. [1]

I have noticed my pet is drinking less water daily. Should I be concerned?

No, this is completely to be expected. Raw food already contains the moisture necessary for digestion. Because kibble has had the water removed, dogs constantly have to drink water in an attempt to maintain proper hydration. Water is one of the most basic of requirements of all living things. Our pets need to be well hydrated so their bodies can function optimally.

My pet has existing health problems. Can they still eat raw?

In most cases your pet will be able to eat a raw diet. In fact you will likely see an improvement of their health after they are eating raw. For advice specific to your pet I would suggest using the services of a professional well versed in natural health and nutrition.

What is the best way to travel with a raw fed animal?

If you are travelling by car you can take an extra cooler. Freeze meals in separate portions so you can take one meal out at a time. If taking a cooler is not feasible you can purchase food along the way. In a pinch dehydrated raw could be fed or mixed with fresh raw food.

I forgot to defrost food. What should I do?

Make it a fast day. Or feed whole raw eggs and a frozen meaty bone. Do not defrost food in the microwave. It changes the molecular structure of food and can cook bones, making them dangerous for the animal to eat.

Do high protein diets cause growth problems?

There is a misconception that a raw diet is high in protein. This is not true. A fresh raw diet contains between 15%-22% protein. Unlike dry kibble, animal tissues are made of up mostly water, around 60-70%. To check the protein content of a type of raw meat you can look it up online on the USDA nutrient database. What does have the potential to create growth problems is excess calories that allow the animal to become overweight, and an excess or deficiency of calcium. A varied raw diet promotes steady even growth.

Grain & legume based diets contain phosphorus in the form of phytic acid, which is not readily available to carnivores. So although the levels of phosphorus and calcium may look adequate on paper, they are in actuality often insufficient to meet the needs of growing animals resulting in a nutritional deficiency, leading to skeletal disease. [1]

Why doesn't my vet advocate feeding a raw diet?

In veterinary school students are taught that dogs are omnivores by "experts" from the pet food industry. Throughout their years of education, it is not unusual to spend as little as two days on the subject of companion animal nutrition. What little education they do receive on nutrition is often taught by experts working in the processed food industry. They are warned that feeding raw meat is risky because of bacterial contamination. The experts from the pet food companies benefit financially when veterinarian's promote their foods. Laboratory experiments and testing are relied upon to make the case for processed foods instead of actual long term feeding trials like Pottinger's study on cats.

The "danger" of bacteria in raw meat is often the first thing the pet owner is warned about when it comes to a raw diet. Interestingly, conventional healthcare also seeks to destroy bacteria in the body by using antibiotics. Our society has been made to be fearful of all bacteria, when we should be instead concerned with creating healthy strong bodies that are unable to be overcome by bacteria as should naturally occur.

Student veterinarians are also told that selling processed pet food is a good way to bring money to the bottom line. Seeing as most veterinarians have a considerable debt load upon graduation, earning money becomes a big priority. The veterinary associations are also against raw feeding. One might guess this position was taken because of pressure from powerful pet food companies.

People become vets because of a love for animals and a desire to help them. Yet the education they receive turns them away from a path of true healing. I do believe most of them truly do care about animals and want to improve their health, but that they have become misguided because of their education.

Since many pet owners are learning about the benefits of raw feeding and choosing this diet for their pets it is being brought out into the open much more. There are veterinarians who have pursued further education on the topic of nutrition and do advocate feeding a raw diet. The bottom line though, is that most vets do not receive adequate education in nutrition and therefore lack the qualifications to even make diet recommendations.

"Nature can do more than physicians"
~Jean Louis Agassiz

14
Animal Naturopathy

I wanted to devote a chapter to this subject and how it relates to raw feeding as the two go hand in hand. Species appropriate diets are but one part of a bigger picture in regards to natural pet care.

Naturopathy follows laws set out by nature in order to prevent disease and promote health. This type of care can be applied to animals and people alike. But naturopathy is more than following the laws of nature. It is a philosophy, and a way of life, a lifelong way of being.

The Merriam-Webster dictionary defines naturopathy as: *a system of treatment of disease that avoids drugs and surgery and emphasizes the use of natural agents (as air, water, and herbs) and physical means (as tissue manipulation and electrotherapy).* [1]

Even though the term naturopathy was coined in 1895, the beliefs associated with it have much older origins. Hippocrates (460 BC – 370 BC) who is referred to as "the father of medicine" believed that disease was a product of environment, diet and living habits. His therapeutic approach was based on "the healing power of nature".

Our society seems to think that human ingenuity can be more efficient than nature. But nature is not flawed in any way. Everything fits together in a perfect puzzle. When we try to go against the laws of nature to make food grow faster, to stave off symptoms of ill health or to make our lives more convenient we must deal with the multitude of negative consequences of those actions.

All the keys to great health are found in nature. Our culture has been taught quite a lot of misinformation for some time now on the subject of health. This is especially true in North America. When we ask the questions and seek the truth for ourselves we will find that the answers have been right there in nature the entire time. We merely need to be open to seeing them.

Modern medicine is otherwise known as allopathic care. The Merriam-Webster dictionary defines allopathic as: *relating to or being a system of medicine that aims to combat disease by using remedies (as drugs or surgery) which produce effects that are different from or incompatible with those of the disease being treated.* [1]

The standard treatment system of veterinary medicine is also allopathic and does not make our pets well in most cases.

Symptoms are treated with drugs, which in turn cause other symptoms, which result in further drugs being prescribed. Tumors and diseased tissue are physically removed. Why is the cause not searched for? Never mind actually acting to remove the cause. Drugs weaken the body, destroy beneficial bacteria, overload the animal with toxins and cause permanent damage to the organs. The animal in this weakened state no longer has the strength to efficiently deal with pathogens, bacteria, parasites & viruses that it comes into contact with during its daily life. It is a vicious cycle.

The elimination of a symptom is not the elimination of the disease. In both humans and animals, symptoms are the way our bodies communicate that something we are doing is not good for us. It is a warning that lifestyle changes are needed to return to a state of health.

Has the desire for wealth perpetuated the current methods of veterinary science? Ask yourself who stands to gain when pets are ill? Is the affiliation between veterinarian's, pharmaceutical companies and pet food companies in our pets best interests? Is the affiliation even ethical? Look at the connections between these groups and how they contribute to each other's success in business. Who is benefiting from these partnerships? And who is suffering because of them?

It's only when we act in harmony with nature that we will enable prevention of disease and promotion of health. By putting the laws of health into practice for our animals we are setting the stage for optimal health. Unlike allopathic care, naturopathic treatment is centered on the cause of the symptom to affect a long-term cure. These naturopathic principles will give your animals absolutely everything they require to experience great health.

Why would pet owners choose to use the services of a veterinary naturopath? Let's explore what a veterinary naturopath does and the benefits of accessing their services.

There are six fundamental principles that all naturopaths follow:

The healing power of nature
    - use the body's innate ability to heal itself
Identify and address the cause
    -look beyond symptoms to the underlying cause
First do no harm
    -use methods that are non-invasive and have minimal side effects
Doctor as teacher
    -educate clients about the ways to achieve optimal health for their pets
Target the whole
    -all aspects of the animal are taken into account (physical, mental & emotional)
Prevention is the best cure
    -focus on building health rather than treating disease [2]

The role of naturopathic practitioners is to provide their clients with the knowledge that will enable them to take control of their pet's health and support them through this process.

To facilitate optimal health, naturopaths follow the laws of nature and employ non-invasive healing modalities that focus on the animal as a whole. Pet owners can seek out a naturopathic practitioner as the first step to promoting health in their pets. Naturopaths excel at addressing chronic health conditions. When the animal has been given proper nutrition, exercise, fresh water, fresh air, exposure to sun and sufficient rest the natural balance is restored and healing will take place. An assortment of remedies may be used to support healing such as: homeopathy, massage, essential oils, herbs, and hydrotherapy. Naturopaths do not diagnose disease, prescribe drugs or perform surgery.

Because naturopathic care looks at the animal as a whole, practitioners will ask for a lot of detailed information about your pet. Based on the information collected, a health plan will be developed for the animal. With the naturopath for support, the pet owner will be in charge of putting the plan into action. Instead of treating individual symptoms, the naturopath addresses the cause of a health issue. Only when the cause is addressed can true healing take place. However this will not happen overnight. The body has deteriorated over time, and the healing will also happen over a period of time.

There are many reasons that individuals seek out the services of naturopaths. Their conventional veterinarian may have exclaimed that there is nothing further that they can do for the animal, costly drugs are not producing the desired results, the condition keeps returning, the owners are concerned about the side effects of drugs, naturopathy is in alignment with the owner's beliefs, or the owner wants to be proactive and prevent health issues in their pet.

The laws of nature work in unison to create a perfect balance of health. They are easy to understand and put into practice for your animals. By using a naturopathic approach we can prevent disease from developing in our animals in the first place, giving them a fantastic quality of life and saving ourselves much heartache and thousands of dollars in the process. Preventing a health condition from developing is so much easier than trying to remedy it once it has developed. Pet owners could save themselves so much grief by simply being proactive with their pet's health.

Henry Lindlahr (1862 – 1924) further developed the "Nature Cure" system of natural healing into a more comprehensive system he called "Natural Therapeutics". Lindlahr stated that the primary cause of disease is violation of nature's laws and acute disease is the result of a cleansing and healing effort of nature. He believed that only when we are in compliance with nature's laws would we have the ability to attain and maintain perfect health. [3]

Lindlahr disagreed with the allopathic method of suppressing symptoms. He compares symptom suppression to cutting the top off of a weed. The weed is no longer seen, but it has not been eliminated. It lurks just under the surface only to sprout up again. Conventional veterinarians will generally prescribe a drug to combat any unwelcome symptoms. The symptoms go away and we think our pet is cured. In reality the drugs have halted nature's attempt of self healing. Keeping the weed analogy in mind, we could imagine that once the top is cut off, the roots start to spread out underground without being seen and in short order we will see new shoots of the weed sprouting up in multiple different areas. While it temporarily looked like the weed was gone, we see that it has come back stronger than ever. [3]

Conventional veterinary medicine includes vaccinations, flea & tick control, pre-packaged processed food, drugs, and more drugs. Everything that we give to our pets which they ingest, absorb in their skin or we inject into them has a direct effect on their health. The poisons and toxins in these products build up in the organs and tissues of our pets. This weakens them and creates a cycle of illness.

The Banfield Pet Hospital released a report in 2012 documenting pet health statistics based on over 2 million dogs and 430,000 cats treated during 2011 in 43 different states. The report shows that chronic disease and obesity are on the rise. Less than 30% of dogs aged between 1 and 3 years and only 13% of mature dogs (3-10 years of age) were diagnosed as healthy. I feel these statistics representing our pets are a huge problem, 70% of young adult dogs should not have health issues. This overwhelming rate of disease is very preventable. [4]

Cancer is now one of the top causes of death in both pets and humans. Henry Lindlahr wrote that dogs are more often afflicted with malignant tumors than are other animals due to sharing man's food and receiving just as much doctoring as their owners do. [3]

Lindlahr also goes into some detail regarding the hereditary factor of cancer. He agrees that cancer has been proven to be hereditary. However, his stance is that this is due to the fetus being a multiplication of the already abnormal parent cell (due to environmental pollution) and that the diseased constituents of the cell will reproduce themselves in the offspring. The diseased constituents are caused by an unhealthy lifestyle. [3] The type of care our pets receive affecting their health, it's also influencing future generations.

The field of epigenetics is a growing area of study. It is the study of how environment affects the way genes are expressed in the body. Changes in how genes are expressed can be passed onto future generations even though there has been no change in the actual DNA. We have the power to stop this now. We can give our animals back their health. But with each generation of illness being carried forward this task grows increasingly difficult.

We now also see a lot of autoimmune diseases in both humans and in pets. These diseases are rarely if ever seen in wild animals. Wild animals are not getting vaccinated, are eating a species appropriate diet, and are outdoors getting fresh air, water, exercise and sunshine. It is not difficult to see the differences in lifestyles between wild and domestic animals. So then is it not clear what direction we must move in to improve the health of our pets? We need to model their care after the lifestyle of their wild brethren. This doesn't mean we shouldn't provide our animals with the comfort and benefits of our care compared to the sometimes harsh lives of wild animals. But we need to ensure that we stay true to their species specific needs.

Conventional veterinary medicine has made great progress in diagnostics, surgical techniques and acute care but the treatment of chronic diseases in pets is not overly effective. This should be obvious upon an honest evaluation of the health of today's pets. The shortcomings of a system based on drugs and surgery leaves a lot to be desired. But if we take action, we can ultimately reverse the state of illness that our pets as a whole are experiencing.

Nutrition is the cornerstone of naturopathy. Our animals can only function at their best when they are eating a species appropriate diet. Pet owners desperately need to take a hard look at what they are feeding their animals and get educated on the facts. A bowl of over processed dried, preserved "food" made of animal products, grains & vegetables with sprayed on flavor enhancers is never what nature intended dogs and cats to eat.

You can take an active role in your pet's health by learning how to promote health and prevent disease and then putting that knowledge into action through diet and lifestyle.

"Thousands upon thousands of persons have studied disease. Almost no one has studied health"
~Adelle Davis

15
Veterinarian Visits

I have encountered many raw feeders that have a great deal of trepidation when faced with the possibility of discussing their pet's diet with a veterinarian. No one wants to be chastised for his or her pet care choices if the veterinarian happens to disagree with the practice of feeding raw. What is the best way to navigate the pet owner / veterinarian relationship?

First of all you must keep in mind that the veterinarian works for YOU. You are paying them for their advice and services based on their education and experience. You are not obligated to follow through with their recommendations. You are in the position of control, not the veterinarian. Professionals should be accessed to provide information, not to make choices for the client. But I see that many pet owners have given up this control and only rely upon the veterinarian's opinion without seeking other information or viewpoints or even asking questions.

I feel pet owners should be honest about what they are feeding their pet if asked. What should you do if the veterinarian goes off on a tirade about the "dangers" of raw feeding? I would advise not getting into a debate on the subject. Chances are slim to none that you will change the veterinarians mind on the topic. I would suggest explaining that you have researched the topic extensively and have come to the conclusion that this is the best diet for your pet and that you are comfortable with the possible risks of this choice. This communicates that you haven't made this decision on a whim and you understand the possible risks. It also implies that you are not interested in being lectured about the "dangers of raw feeding". Agree to disagree if necessary. If you are able to, research different veterinarian's in your area ahead of time to find one that has become educated on species appropriate diets for companion animals.

Veterinarians are just as susceptible to pet food marketing as any other person on the planet. Having a degree in veterinary medicine in no way makes them immune from the influence of marketing. Pet food companies influence veterinary students by providing educational materials about their brands of food right in the universities and promote their food in vet clinics. This is all about keeping and maintaining their market share. Many pet owners are more likely to choose a food that is recommended by a veterinarian. Yet most veterinarians have minimal education in canine and feline nutrition.

The veterinarians who have diligently studied the topic of animal nutrition are the ones who advocate for feeding a natural diet. Seek them out for your own pet's care.

"Choices made, whether bad or good, follow you forever and affect everyone in their path one way or another"
~J.E.B. Spredemann

16
Your Path

The diet of our companion animals has far reaching consequences upon their health. For better or worse, every single cell in their body is affected by the food they consume each day. Following the evidence that is found from studying anatomy, physiology and evolution will make it obvious what cats and dogs are meant to be eating.

Understanding firstly that processed foods are a cause of illness in pets and secondly that improvements will not be made unless a cause of illness is removed should show you that to promote health the diet is essential.

I urge you not to wait until your pet develops a health problem before you find the motivation to feed them a species appropriate diet. Much of the damage caused by processed foods will have lasting effects on the animal's health. Ideally an animal that has been naturally raised from birth, from parents that were naturally raised will be the best source for a long lived healthy companion.

Realize that the advertising we are continually bombarded with for pet foods has little to do with the animals and everything to do with money. We simply need to look at the actions or lack of action in many instances concerning pet food corporations and the truth concerning their motivation becomes crystal clear. By reading this book you are well on your way to being an informed consumer.

Be a truth seeker and an advocate for your animals! Domestic animals rely on us as their guardians, to speak for them and make decisions that are in their best interests. Only when we are educated on the facts are we in the position to make good decisions. Recognize that the facts will not be found from those who stand to personally gain from the outcome of your decision.

If you find yourself stuck with a situation with your animal (deciding if a certain food is appropriate for example) just ask yourself "what would the situation be if this was a wild carnivore?" and "how would things play out if I wasn't here to care for this animal?" It is a simple question, but it has helped me immensely by reminding me of the qualities which are inherent to the animal and showing me the way to honor the carnivore residing within all the cats and dogs I have cared for.

For further reading on the topic of species appropriate nutrition I recommend:

Work Wonders: Feed Your Dog Raw Meaty Bones
Tom Lonsdale, DVM

Raw Fed Cats
Linda Zurich

For further reading on related natural pet care topics:

Mark of the Beast: Hidden in Plain Sight
Patricia Jordan, DVM

Homeopathic Care for Dogs and Cats
Don Hamilton, DVM

The Complete Herbal Handbook for the Dog and Cat
Juliette de Bairacli Levy

Wild Health: Lessons in Natural Wellness from the Animal Kingdom
Cindy Engel

To find a naturally raised dog visit The Natural Rearing Breeder's Association on the web:
http://nrbreedersassociation.wordpress.com/

For a listing of both dog and cat breeders who incorporate natural care with their animals visit Natural Rearing at
http://www.naturalrearing.com/coda/index.html#landing

References

1 Anatomy Dictates Diet
1 Swenson, J. (2000) *Action plan for the conservation of the brown bear in Europe*; Council of Europe; Tungasletta, Norway.
2 Stirling, I. (1988) *The first polar bears*; Polar Bears; Ann Arbor; University of Michigan Press; Ann Arbor, MI

The Point of Entry
1 Chistiansen, P. & Wroe, S. (2007) *Bite forces and evolutionary adaptation to feeding ecology in carnivores*; Journal of Ecology; Vol 88, issue 2
2 Ewer, R. (1998) *The Carnivores*; Cornell University Press; Ithaca, NY
3 Stegemann, E. (2006) *Skull science*; NYS Department of Environmental Conservation; Albany, NY
4 Wang, X. & Tedford, R. (2008) *Dogs: Their fossil relatives & evolutionary history*; Columbia University Press; New York, NY
5 Feldhamer, G. (1999) *Mammology: adaptation, diversity and ecology*, 1st Edition; WCB/McGraw-Hill; Boston, MA
6 Crossley, D. (1995) *Tooth enamel thickness in the mature dentition of domestic dogs and cats – preliminary study*; Journal of Veterinary Dentistry; 12; 111-113
7 Li X., Li W., Wang H., Bayley D., Cao J.,... Brand, J. (2006) *Cats lack a sweet taste receptor*; Journal of Nutrition; vol. 136 no. 7 1932S-1934S
8 Moore A., Choron S., Choron H. (2007) *Planet cat*; Houghton Mifflin Harcourt; Orlando, FL
9 Case, L. (2013) *The dog: its behavior, nutrition and health*; John Wiley & Sons; Mississauga, ON
10 Denny, M. & McFadzean, A. (2011) *Engineering animals*; Harvard University Press; Cambridge, MA
11 Taylor, P. (2010) *Running dog maintenance*; Skycat Publications; Lavenham, Suffolk, UK
12 Grandjean, D. & Vasaire, J. (2002) *The royal canin dog encyclopedia*; Aniwa Publishing, Aniwa, WI

Down the Hatch
1 Feldhamer, G., Drickamer, L., Vessey, S., Merrit, J., Krajewski, J. (2007) *Mammology: adaptation, diversity, ecology*; JHU Press; Baltimore, MD

2 Grandjean, D. & Vasaire, J. (2002) *The royal canin dog encyclopedia;* Aniwa Publishing; Aniwa, WI
3 Lonsdale, T. (2001) Raw meaty bones promote health; Rivetco P/L; NSW, AU
4 National Research Council (2006) *Nutrient requirements of dogs and cats;* The National Academies Press; Washington, DC
5 National Research Council (2006) *Nutrient requirements of dogs and cats;* The National Academies Press; Washington, DC
6 Burger, I. & Rivers, J. (1989) *Nutrition of the dog and cat*; Cambridge University Press; Cambridge, England
7 Agar, S. (2008) *Small animal nutrition*; Butterworth-Heinemann; London, UK
8 National Research Council (2006) *Nutrient requirements of dogs and cats;* The National Academies Press; Washington, DC
9 Case, L., Daristotle, L., Hayek, M., Foess Raasch, M. (2011) *Canine and feline nutrition: a resource for companion animal professionals*; Mosby Inc.; Maryland Heights, MO

Comparing Digestive Anatomy
1 Feldhamer, G., Drickamer, L., Vessey, S., Merrit, J., Krajewski, J. (2007) *Mammology: adaptation, diversity, ecology*; JHU Press; Baltimore, MD
2 Burger, I. & Rivers, J. (1989) *Nutrition of the dog and cat: Waltham Symposium Number 7*; Cambridge University Press; New York, NY
3 Merritt, J. (2010) *The biology of small mammals*; JHU Press; Baltimore, MD
4 Bouyet, B. (2002) *Akita, treasure of Japan*, Volume 2; Magnum Publishing; Thousand Oaks, CA
5 Guth, S. (2009) *How dogs digest different foods*; NZ Dog World; New Zealand Kennel Club
6 Snyder, K. (2011) *The beauty detox solution*; Harlequin; Buffalo, NY
7 Gowans, S. (2005) *Ayurvedic cooking;* Jaico Publishing House; Mumbai, India
8 Fuller, M. (2004) *The encyclopedia of farm animal nutrition*; CABI Publishing; Cambridge, MA
9 Shears, R. (2009) *The castaway dog who swam six miles through shark-infested waters, then survived four months on a desert island*; Daily Mail; Retrieved September 10, 2013 from:

http://www.dailymail.co.uk/news/article-1167967/The-castaway-dog-swam-SIX-miles-shark-infested-waters-survived-FOUR-months-desert-island.html

Wild Bretheren

1 Cantwell, M (2012) *Good puppy academics: Using nature's way to raise your dog's gpa*; Xlibris; Bloomington, IN

2 Hendriks, W. (2013) Waltham international nutritional sciences symposium; Waltham; Retrieved November 20, 2013 from: http://www.waltham.com/news/waltham-international-nutritional-sciences-symposium-2013.shtml

3 Mech, D. (1981) *The wolf: The ecology and behavior of an endangered species*; University Of Minnesota Press; 1st edition; Minneapolis, MN

4 Lopez, B. (1978) *Of wolves and men*, McMillan Publishing, New York, NY

5 Mech, D. (1981) *The wolf: The ecology and behavior of an endangered species*; University Of Minnesota Press; 1st edition; Minneapolis, MN

6 Muller, S. (2012) *Diet composition of wolves (Canis lupus) on the Scandinavian Peninsula determined by scat analysis*; Retrieved November 27, 2013 from: www.rufford.org/files/10233-1 Detailed Final Report_0.pdf

7 Reed, J., Ballard, W., Gipson, P., Kelly, B., Krausman, P. Wallace, M. Webster, D. (2006) *Diets of free-ranging Mexican Gray wolves in Arizona and New Mexico*, Wildlife Society Bulletin.

8 Knappwost, U. (2006) *Territorial variation in the wolves diet? A comparison of 11 territories in Sweden*; Retrieved November 27, 2013 from: http://www1.nina.no/RovviltPub/pdf/Summary-Dipl.Terr.Var.UKnappworst.pdf

9 Darwin, C. (1975) *Charles Darwin's natural selection*; Cambridge University Press; New York, NY

10 Driscoll, C. (2007) *The near eastern origin of cat domestication*; Journal of Science Vol. 317; American Association for the advancement of science; Washington, DC

11 Heptner, V. & Sludskii, A. (1992) *Mammals of the Soviet Union: Carnivora (hyenas and cats),* Vol. 2. Smithsonian Institution Libraries and National Science Foundation.

12 Lonsdale, T. (2001) *Raw meaty bones promote health*; Rivetco P/L; NSW, AU

13 Engel, C. (2002) *Wild health: Lessons in natural wellness from the animal kingdom*; Houghton Mifflin; New York, NY

2 The Early Days of Feeding Cats and Dogs
1 Terentius M. (n.d.) *Rerum Rusticarum Libri Tres.(Three books on farming)*
2 Gaston III, Comte de (1871) *Livre de Chasse;* Johanssons boktr.
3 Robinson, H. (1879) *The great fur land or sketches of life in the Hudson's Bay Territory;* G.P. Putnam's Sons; New York.
4 Nestle, M. & Nesheim, M. (2010) *Feed your pet right: The authoritative guide to feeding the dog and cat*; Free Press; New York, NY
5 Nestle, M. & Nesheim, M. (2010) *Feed your pet right: The authoritative guide to feeding the dog and cat*; Free Press; New York, NY

3 Evolution of Pet Food
1 Lonsdale, T. (2001) *Raw meaty bones promote health*; Rivetco P/L; NSW, AU
2 Coghlan, J. (2012) *Paleopet: The real reason our dog or cat eats grass*; Booktango; Bloomingtom, IN
3 Phillips, T. (2007) *Learn from the past*; Pet Food Industry Magazine; Retrieved September 18, 2013 from: http://www.petfoodindustry.com/3901.html
4 Nestle, M. & Nesheim, M. (2010) *Feed your pet right: the authoritative guide to feeding your dog and cat*; Free Press; New York, NY
5 Phillips, T. (2007) *Learn from the past*; Pet Food Industry; Retrieved September 18, 2013 from: http://www.petfoodindustry.com/3901.html
6 Hills Pet Nutrition (n.d.) The story of Hills Pet Nutrition; Hills Pet Nutrition; Retrieved September 10, 2013 from: http://www.hillspet.com/our-company/story-of-hills-pet-nutrition.html
7 Lonsdale, T. (2001) *Raw meaty bones promote health*; Rivetco P/L; NSW, AU
8 Phillips, T. (2007) *Learn from the past*; Pet Food Industry; Retrieved September 18, 2013 from: http://www.petfoodindustry.com/3901.html

Origins of Raw Feeding
Industry Organizations
1 Lonsdale, T. (2001) *Raw meaty bones promote health*; Rivetco P/L; NSW, AU
2 Bouyet, B. (2002) *Akita, treasure of Japan*, Volume 2; Magnum Publishing; Thousand Oaks, CA

3 Association of American Feed Control Officials (2007) *Official publication*; Regulation PE3, 120–121
4 Lonsdale, T. (2001) *Raw meaty bones promote health*; Rivetco P/L; NSW, AU
5 Bouyet, B. (2002) *Akita, treasure of Japan*, Volume 2; Magnum Publishing; Thousand Oaks, CA

4 Processed Pet Foods Impair Health
1 Lee, J. (2012) *Kibble is inflicting serious harm on our pets*; Raw Instinct Magazine Vol. 1 Issue 10.

Not Species Appropriate
1 Jordan, P. (n.d.) Feeding the carnivore companion; Revtreived jan 30, 2014 from: http://dr-jordan.com/wp-content/uploads/2013/04/Carnivore-Companion2-By-Dr.-Patricia-Jordan.pdf
2 Lonsdale, T. (2001) *Raw meaty bones promote health*; Rivetco P/L; NSW, AU

Harmful Ingredients
1 Martin, A. (1997) *Foods pets die for*; New Sage Press; Troutdale, OR
2 U.S. Federal Drug Administration (2002) *Food and Drug Administration/Center for Veterinary Medicine Report on the risk from Phenobarbital in pet food*; Retrieved October 1, 2013 from: http://www.fda.gov/AboutFDA/CentersOffices/OfficeofFoods/CVM/CVMFOIAElectronicReadingRoom/ucm129131.htm
3 Stein, D. (1994) *Natural remedy book for dogs and cats*; Random House LLC; New York, NY
4 Bouyet, B. (2002) *Akita, treasure of Japan*, Volume 2; Magnum Publishing; Thousand Oaks, CA
5 Lee, J. (2012) *Kibble is inflicting serious harm on our pets*; Raw Instincts Magazine Vol. 1 Issue 10.
6 Bouyet, B. (2002) *Akita, treasure of Japan, Volume 2*; Magnum Publishing; Thousand Oaks, CA
7 Atkins, P., Ernyei, L., Driscoll, W., Obenauf, R., Thomas, R. (2011) *Analysis of toxin trace metals in pet foods using cryogenic grinding and quantitation b ICP-MS part II*; Spectrocopy Magazine (26) 2
8 Dodds, G. (n.d.) Heavy metal poisoning and hair analysis (part 1) Retrieved January 31, 2013 from: http://www.holisticvetpetcare.com/heavy_metal_posion.htm
9 Balagapolan, C. (1988) *Cassava in food, feed, and industry*; CRC Press; Boca Raton, FL

10 Nahrer, K. (2013) *Mycotoxins – A risk for companion animals?* Biomin; Retrieved September 22, 2013 from: http://www.biomin.net/index.php?id=62&type=123&L=0&tx_ttnews[tt_news]=721&cHash=731b270a25fc0d84273d81834d9d0224

Processing

1 Martin, A. (1997) *Foods pets die for*; New Sage Press; Troutdale, OR
2 Morgan, A. & Kern, G. (1933) *The effect of heat upon the biological value of meat protein*; Laboratory of Household Science, University of California; Berkley, CA
3 Lonsdale, T. (2001) *Raw meaty bones promote health*; Rivetco P/L; NSW, AU
4 Elkins, R. (1998) *Digestive enzymes: The key to good health and longevity*; Woodland Publishing; Pleasant Grove, UT
5 Agar, S. (2008) *Small animal nutrition*; Butterworth-Heinemann; London
6 Lonsdale, T. (2001) *Raw meaty bones promote health*; Rivetco P/L; NSW, AU
7 Pottinger, F. (1995) *Pottinger's cats: a study in nutrition*; Price-Pottinger Nutrition Foundation Inc.; Lemon Grove, CA

Digestibility

1 CBC Marketplace (2012) *Pet food: a dog's breakfast;* Retrieved September 27, 2013 from: http://www.youtube.com/watch?v=GrBOOhDCC6g
2 Agar, S. (2008) *Small animal nutrition*; Butterworth-Heinemann; London, UK
3 Guth, S. (2009) *How dogs digest different foods*; NZ Dog World; New Zealand Kennel Club

Recalls

1 Center's for Disease Control and Prevention (2012) *Multi-state outbreak of human salmonella infantis infections linked to dry dog food (Final update)*; Retrieved October 3, 2013 from: http://www.cdc.gov/salmonella/dog-food-05-12/index.html

Marketing

1 Fascetti, J. & Delaney, S. (2012) *Applied veterinary clinical nutrition*; 3rd Edition; Wiley-Blackwell; West Sussex, UK
2 Lee, J. (2012) *Dogs are carnivores not kibblevore's*; Raw Instinct Magazine; Vol. 1 Issue 8

Effects on Health

1 Lennon, J. (n.d.) *Allergies & nutrition, exactly what is the connection?*; Tolden Farms; Retrieved December 1, 2013 from: http://www.tolldenfarms.ca/reference/101-allergies
2 Tenney, L. (1997) *The natural guide to colon health;* Woodland Publishing; Salt Lake City, UT
3 Schaer, M. (2009) *Clinical medicine of the dog and cat*; Manson Publishing; Dubai, UAE
4 Lonsdale, T. (2001) *Raw meaty bones promote health*; Rivetco P/L; NSW, AU
5 Fougere, B. (2006) *The pet lover's guide to natural healing for dogs and cats*; Elsevier Health Sciences; St Louis, MO
6 Symes, B. (2010) *Gastric acidity, digesting bones, gut transit time and salmonella*; Vets All Natural; Retrieved November 12, 2013 from: http://www.vetsallnatural.com.au/index.php?option=com_content&view=article&id=107&Itemid=113
7 Logan, E., Wiggs, R. Zetner, K., Hefferren, J. (2000) *Dental disease in small animal clinical nutrition, Fourth Edition; Morris Institute;* Topeka, KS
8 Ewer, R. (1973) *The carnivores*; Cornell University Press; Ithaca, NY
9 National Research Council (2006) *Nutrient requirements of dogs and cats;* The National Academies Press; Washington, DC
10 Kent C. (2013) *What you need to know about kibble*; Dogs Naturally Magazine; Ontario, Canada.
11 Seefelt S. & Chapman T. (1979) *Body water content and turnover in cats fed dry and canned rations*; Am J Vet Res, 40(2): 183–5
12 Hodgkins, E. (n.d.) *Your diabetic cat*; Retrieved October 13, 2013 from: http://yourdiabeticcat.com/
13 The Association for Pet Obesity Prevention (n.d.); Retrieved October 9, 2013 from: http://www.petobesityprevention.com/pet-obesity-fact-risks/
14 Hoffman, M. (1998) *Dogs: The ultimate care guide*; Rodale Books; Emmaus, PA
15 Bouyet, B. (2002) *Akita, treasure of Japan*, Volume 2; Magnum Publishing; Thousand Oaks, CA

5 Sourcing and Storing Raw Foods
1 Lee, J. (2013) *Getting ready for a new puppy: sourcing and storing raw food*; Raw Instincts Magazine; Vol. 2, Issue 11
Direct from the Farm
Roadkill

Processing a Carcass
Storing Raw Food
1 Lee, J. (2013) *Getting ready for a new puppy: sourcing and storing raw food*; Raw Instincts Magazine; Vol. 2, Issue 11
2 Oster, K. (2011) *The complete guide to preserving meat, fish and game*; Atlantic Publishing Company; Ocala, FL
6 What & Where to Feed
Size of Foods
Organs
Tripe
1 Scott, D. (2010) *The stink on tripe*; Dogs Naturally Magazine Vol. 1 Issue 6; Breton, ON
Fat
1 Coffman, M. (n.d.) *Feeding the high performance bird dog*; University of Florida
2 Brown, S. (2009) *Unlocking the canine ancestral diet*; Dogwise Publishing; Wenatchee, WA
3 Coghlan, J. (2012) *Paleopet: The real reason our dog or cat eats grass*; Booktango; Bloomingtom, IN
Fish
Eggs
1 Mercola, J. (2000) *Don't be chicken of the egg;* Journal of the American College of Nutrition
2 Canion, P. (2012) *Do you know nutrition: egg shell membrane a rich source of calcium;* Victoria Advocate; Victoria, B.C.
3 Lonsdale, T. (2005). *Work wonders: Feed your dog raw meaty bones;* Rivetco P/L; NSW, AU
Raw Bones
1 Bouyet, B. (2002) *Akita, treasure of Japan*, Volume 2; Magnum Publishing; Thousand Oaks, CA
2 Pitcairn, R. (2005) *Dr. Pitcairn's new complete guide to natural health for dogs and cats*; Rodale Inc; Emmaus, PA
3 Mahgoub, O., Kadim, I., Webb, E. (2012) *Goat meat production and quality*; CABI, Oxfordshire, UK
4 Pond, W., (2004) *Encyclopedia of animal science*; CRC Press, New York, NY
Whole Prey
Muscle Meat
Other Parts

Enhanced Meat
Freezer Burnt Meat
Expired Meat
Ground Meat
Frozen Meat
Fruit, Veggies, Grains & Dairy
1 Mech, D. & Boitani, L. (2007) *Wolves: Behavior, ecology and conservation*; University Of Chicago Press; 1st edition; Chicago, IL
2 Agar, S. (2008) *Small animal nutrition*; Butterworth-Heinemann; London, UK
3 Boyd, D. (1998) *Herbivores busted preying on bird nests*; Casper Star Tribune; Casper, WY
4 Kronfeld, D. (1978) *Home cooking for dogs*; Pure-Bred Dogs American Kennel Gazette.
5 Kneuven, D. (2013) *Research proves it: Dogs thrive on a starch-rich diet.* Dogs Naturally Magazine; Beeton, ON
6 Bouyet, B. (2002) *Akita, treasure of Japan*, Volume 2; Magnum Publishing; Thousand Oaks, CA
7 Coghlan, J. (2012) *Paleopet: The real reason our dog or cat eats grass*; Booktango; Bloomingtom, IN
8 Lennon, J. (n.d.) *Allergies & nutrition, exactly what is the connection?*; Tolden Farms; Retrieved December 1, 2013 from: http://www.tolldenfarms.ca/reference/101-allergies
9 Jensen, B. (1981) *Tissue Cleansing Through Bowel Management*; Bernard Jensen Intl; San Marcos, CA
10 Lennon, J. (n.d.) *Allergies & nutrition, exactly what is the connection?*; Tolden Farms; Retrieved December 1, 2013 from: http://www.tolldenfarms.ca/reference/101-allergies
Fiber
1 Depauw, S. (2012) *Animal fiber: A key factor in gastrointestinal health in an obligate carnivore: the cheetah*; Ghent University; Merelbeke, Belgium
Treats
Fresh Water
1 Case, L., Daristotle, L., Hayek, M., Foess Raasch, M. (2011) *Canine and feline nutrition: a resource for companion animal professionals*; Mosby Inc.; Maryland Heights, MO
Where to Feed
7 How Much & How Often to Feed

How Much to Feed
1 Lonsdale, T. (2005) *Work wonders: Feed your dog raw meaty bones.* Rivetco P/L; NSW, AU
Calculating Feeding Amounts
How Often to Feed
1 Tams, T. (2003) *Handbook of small animal gastroenterology*; Elsevier Health Sciences; St Louis, MO
2 Lonsdale, T. (2005) *Work wonders: Feed your dog raw meaty bones.* Rivetco P/L; NSW, AU
Fasting
1 Carrington, H. (1963) *Vitality, fasting and nutrition*; Mokelumne Hill Press; Mokelumne Hill, CA
8 Making the Switch
1 Lee J. (2012) *The learning curve of raw feeding*; Raw Instincts Magazine Vol. 1 Issue 11.
Dealing with a Refuser
1 Zurich, L. (2010) *Raw fed cats*
Changes to Expect
Balance over Time
Detoxification and the Healing Crisis
1 Goldstein, M. (2009) The *nature of animal healing: The definitive holistic medicine guide to caring for your dog and cat*; Random House; New York, NY
9 Feeding Puppies and Kittens
1 Agar, S. (2008) *Small animal nutrition*; Butterworth-Heinemann; London, UK
2 Riser W., Cohen D., Lindquist S. (1964) *Influence of early rapid growth and weight gain on hip dysplasia in the German shepherd dog*; J Am Vet Med Assoc 145:661
3 Riser W. & Larsen J. (1974) *Influence of breed somatotypes on the prevalence of hip dysplasia in the dog*; J Am Vet Med Assoc 165:79
4 Riser W. & Shirer J. (1967) *Correlation between canine hip dysplasia and pelvic muscle mass: A study of 95 dogs*; Am J Vet Res 124:769
10 Supplements
11 Knowing the Risks & Dispelling Myth's
1 Stone, R. (2013) *Eliminating pathogens in meat, food safety or overkill?* Dogs Naturally Magazine; Beeton, ON
12 Reaping the Benefits of Raw Feeding

1 Olson, L. (2010) *Raw and natural nutrition for dogs*; North Atlantic Books; Berkeley, CA
2 Fascetti, J. & Delaney, S. (2012) *Applied veterinary clinical nutrition*; Third Edition; Wiley-Blackwell; West Sussex, UK
3 Lennon, J. (n.d.) *Allergies & nutrition, exactly what is the connection?*; Tolden Farms; Retrieved December 1, 2013 from: http://www.tolldenfarms.ca/reference/101-allergies
4 Davies, S. (2012) *Parallel universe*; Xlibris Corporation; Bloomington, IN

13 F.A.Q.'S

Aren't bones a hazard to my pet?
My pet is having less frequent bowel movements and they turn white. Is this normal?
Can Bacteria on raw meat make my pet or family sick?
1 Ettinger, S. and Feldman E. (1995) *Textbook of veterinary internal medicine,* 4th Edition. Harcourt Brace; Orlando, FL
2 Hand, M., Thatcher, C., Remillard, R., and Roudebush P. (2000*) Small animal clinical nutrition*; Mark Morris Institute; Topeka, KS
3 Kintner, L. (1949) *Canine salmonellosis;* J Veterinary Medicine; 44:396-398.
4 Sanchez, S., Hofacre, C., Lee, M., Maurer, J. and Doyle, M. (2002) *Animal sources of salmonellosis in humans*; JAVMA 2002; 221:492-497.
Can I feed table scraps?
Can a raw diet reduce the risk of bloat in my dog?
1 Lonsdale, T. (2001) *Raw meaty bones promote health*; Rivetco P/L; NSW, AU
I have noticed my pet is drinking less water daily. Should I be concerned?
My pet has existing health problems. Can they still eat raw?
What is the best way to travel with a raw fed animal?
I forgot to defrost food. What should I do?
Do high protein diets cause growth problems?
1 Agar, S. (2008) *Small animal nutrition*; Butterworth-Heinemann; London, UK
1 Bouyet, B. (2002) *Akita, treasure of Japan*, Volume 2; Magnum Publishing; Thousand Oaks, CA
2 Knueven, D. (2007) *The case for whole foods*; Integrative Veterinary Care Journal Issue V311

3 Agar, S. (2008) *Small animal nutrition*; Butterworth-Heinemann; London, UK

4 Schultze, K. (1998) *The ultimate diet: Natural nutrition for dogs and cats*; Affenbar Ink.

Why doesn't my vet advocate feeding a raw diet?

14 Animal Naturopathy

1 Merriam-Webster Inc (2005) *The merriam webster dictionary*; Perfect Learning Corporation; Logan, IA

2 Bloomer, K., Thomason, T., Hubbard T. (2007) *Naturopathy: Natural healing for our animals*; Animal Talk Naturally. Retrieved November 15, 2013 from:
http://www.animaltalknaturally.com/2007/07/03/naturopathy-natural-healing-for-our-animals-show-101/

3 Lindlahr, H. (1919) *Philosophy of natural therapeutics;* Random House; London, UK

4 Bannfield Pet Hospital (2012) *State of pet health, 2012 report*. Retrieved September 29, 2013 from:
http://www.stateofpethealth.com/

15 Veterinarian Visits

16 Your Path

About the Author

Jennifer Lee lives in rural Alberta, Canada with her husband and their many animal companions. She is a Carnivore Nutritionist certified through The American Council of Animal Naturopathy and a natural rearing dog breeder. Jennifer founded her consulting company The Natural Carnivore in 2012 in an effort to teach pet owners about the benefits of species appropriate nutrition and natural pet care. Jennifer is also a regular writer for Raw Instincts Magazine.

For species appropriate nutritional assistance I can be contacted through my website at www.thenaturalcarnivore.com

The Inner Carnivore